International Seattle:
Creating a Globally Competitive Community

Cover photograph by Don Wilson, Port of Seattle

ISBN 0-9638654-0-4

Publication of this final report has been
made possible by a generous grant from

International Seattle:
Creating a Globally Competitive Community

by John Hamer and Bruce Chapman

DISCOVERY INSTITUTE PRESS

Table of Contents

Preface and Summary

Part I: Defining a Globally Competitive Community

1. A Vision of International Seattle   3
2. What Are the Advantages of Global "Citistates"?   4
3. Can a Globally Competitive Community Be Defined?   8
4. How Do Others See Us?   14
5. What Issues Does Internationalism Raise?   19

Part II: Recommendations—A Strategy for a More Globally Competitive Community

10 Priority Steps   25
20 More Steps   40

Part III: Discussion and Debate

1. Does Metropolitan Seattle Need an International Strategy?   65
2. Can Metropolitan Seattle Succeed in the World League?   68
3. What is the Role of New Communications Technologies?   76
4. What is the City Government's Role?   78
5. Can Metropolitan Seattle Learn from European Cities?   80
6. Why Should "Cascadia" Be a Foreign Policy Priority?   82
7. What are the Obstacles and How Do We Overcome Them?   85
8. What Role Can the University of Washington Play?   91

9. What Can the State Government Do?   92

10. How Can the Federal Government Help?   94

Epilogue   97

Advisory Board   99

Acknowledgments

About Discovery Institute   100

About the Authors

Preface

The metropolitan Seattle area, by some criteria, already is one of the most "international" regions in America. But today it is challenged to live up to its reputation—to choose, in the face of cyclical trade and diplomatic uncertainties, the path it has somewhat casually taken so far. As we consider that choice, we may learn enough about our own civic destiny that we will discover lessons of practical benefit to others outside our region, too. That is the hope of this report: a metropolitan Seattle that contributes ideas as well as goods to an increasingly borderless world.

The post-Cold War world is one in which certain metropolitan areas are becoming the new hubs of economic and cultural initiative—taking their places alongside the traditional nation-states and a few fast-evolving international cross-border regions. At the same time, it is likely that those metropolitan regions will prosper most which orient themselves to expanding international economic opportunities— and which make themselves fully competitive in the world at large.

The new metropolitan/global scope of economic activity also dictates a compatible awareness of social, political, educational and cultural institutions. A conscious strategy to link them will prove advantageous, and the changes such an approach entails will prove to be transforming ones for society. That is, they will redirect our thinking as well as the way we do business and conduct our lives. And, in almost all ways, for the better.

Summary

Consider these paradoxes:

❏ Postponed Boeing airplane deliveries, even as our metropolitan area has established itself among the continent's top export regions.

❏ The prospective closure of major consulates and a trade office here, even as several others have newly opened.

❏ Threats to the fulfillment of North American and global dreams of free trade even as our own "Cascadia" dreams of closer cooperation within the Northwest U.S. and Western Canada near realization.

These are some of the complications of internationalism with which the metropolitan Seattle area lives today. They demonstrate how much we are affected—for good and ill—by global affairs. They also underscore the need to come to grips with what we must do as private and public citizens if our area is not only to survive, but thrive.

Today a major international opportunity or danger that comes our way often lacks a metropolitan forum for discussion and response. We also lack a common strategy that can win general acceptance by our congressional delegation, our state government, our counties, our various cities, our ports, our colleges and universities, our common schools, our trade and business associations, our non-profit international organizations, international church and charitable groups, and all the many businesses and individuals of metropolitan Seattle. We do not have a central office to coordinate our growing and common international interests.

Moreover, committed as our many private and civic bodies are to internationalism, a wide global interest is seldom anybody's sole concern. The challenge, therefore, is how to bring our many groups together in a coherent and united force to make us a more successful and competitive international community.

To that end, this report:

1) Describes the advantages of an international strategy.

2) Presents some definitions of a globally competitive community.

3) Reviews how this area is rated by others in terms of international competitiveness.

4) Considers some of the arguments against an international strategy.

5) Proposes a set of recommendations on ways to increase metropolitan Seattle's international competitiveness—and to make our community an even better place to live.

Note our emphasis on "competitive." It's one thing to be considered an "international city," with a cosmopolitan reputation, varied ethnic heritage, tourist attractions and appealing restaurants. But it's quite another to be a truly "globally competitive" metropolis, one that compares favorably anywhere in the world in terms of trade, business, law, finance, infrastructure, education, environment, culture and other vital qualities.

Our recommendations were thus evaluated on this basis: Which ones would most help make the metropolitan Seattle area truly competitive internationally? That's how we arrived at our 10 primary recommendations. Of the other 20 recommendations, many of them could easily have been in the top 10. They do not necessarily appear in order of priority. Some are mainly focused on global competitiveness, while others are more related to international ambience. Both qualities are clearly important, but it seemed to us that these days cities must compete aggressively just to stay even. For example, delegations frequently arrive here asking our most successful local companies to relocate, and offering them strong incentives to do so. Therefore, global competitiveness is not an option, but a necessity. In an ever more unpredictable and contentious world economy, metropolitan regions must have clear strategies in place or they will be left behind.

For metropolitan Seattle, a strategy for global competitiveness should put top emphasis now on an expanded structure for decision-making on international matters—creation of a metropolitan Seattle "foreign office," as it were. We see a need to combine our Seattle area ambitions with those of our true but unofficial international "Sister City"—Vancouver, B.C.—and with the rest of the Pacific Northwest region, often called "Cascadia." Cooperation is also recommended within our metropolitan area when dealing with the development of our seaports, airports and transportation systems. We see as-yet-unrealized economic opportunities in various forms of international tourism (including cruise-ship business), conferences, museums and ethnic activities. Seattle-area citizens will participate best in the new global economy and culture, we hold, if our universities and common schools prepare students better to compete for the real jobs of the future—largely in international trade and high technology, which is itself changing the nature of trade. The community sectors we see as benefiting from at least a partial reorientation to international competitive standards extends from the arts to zoos, and includes one of the defining loyalties of our region, a care for the environment and our quality of life.

This report itself is meant to be a provocative working document for metropolitan Seattle-area decision-makers in government and business who are capable of bringing its recommendations to life. An earlier "Discussion Draft" version of the report served as the catalyst for discussion at a Discovery Institute "International Seattle" conference on May 6, 1993, at the Four Seasons Olympic Hotel in downtown Seattle. That version was revised and edited based on comments and suggestions from the conference's 400 participants. It is both the breadth of the report—that connects trade and commercial issues to opportunities in education, government, and the nonprofit sector—and the prospect of action on the report's recommendations that we hope will best justify the work of so many people.

Part I

*Defining a
Globally Competitive
Community*

1. A Vision of International Seattle

People in and around metropolitan Seattle, typically and optimistically, "want it all." And, on reflection, there is no reason why they shouldn't have it—within reason, anyway.

They want to have secure, prosperous private lives and also enjoy—and contribute to—a robust democratic public life.

They want natural beauty and ecological safety around them, but they also want steady economic growth and a fair chance of career advancement.

They long to preserve the region's trait of friendly, casual intimacy at stores, restaurants and workplaces, but also to be stimulated by contact with the novel, the modern and the exotic in goods and services—and, most of all, people.

Give residents of the central Puget Sound region a guileless, relaxed existence, and yet also offer them a chance to participate in the fascinating and changing world outside our borders, and they'll be happy.

Today, as never before, rapidly changing technology and the global economy that it has enabled can bring us the capacity, if not to "have it all," at least to seek it all. In a time of widespread frustration and even paralysis in many urban areas, it is worth remembering that in this region we really do have the ability to affect our future together in positive ways, to engage in the pursuit of happiness as individuals and as a community.

A new strategy for increasing our region's international competitiveness, which is the subject of this report, provides one promising path toward that goal. It is not the Holy Grail. It won't end hatred, achieve world peace or cure the common cold. Nor is it a late 20th Century revival of the gushing boosterism ("Watch Us Grow!") of the late 19th Century. We know now that bigness is not necessarily goodness, even as we know that some growth seems necessary to making the good life possible.

Rather, an international strategy is an attempt to attach our region's many advantages to the world's best economic and political and cultural trends, and to benefit accordingly.

The "International Seattle" global community we envision in this report is not some steaming polyglot boomtown where we lose the gentle customs and pleasures of our past. On the contrary, we foresee a region that cultivates a keener regard for those very qualities of our pioneer, immigrant and ethnic history which make us distinctive, a region that cooperates better politically, collaborates more sensibly on transportation, and prizes a more attractive and safer environment.

But this vision of a more internationally competitive Seattle also anticipates changes in some popular sensibilities and a sharpening of existing ones. We see a region where, for example:

❏ A sizable portion of our youth will look forward to careers connected to international affairs and commerce, with schooling from elementary years to the university level that reflects this new strategic emphasis.

❏ Regional political and business leaders will be judged in large part on their skill in promoting this area's greater role in the world and on nurturing stronger institutional relations between the public and private sectors.

❏ Metropolitan Seattle is host to numerous international conferences and other events and is seen worldwide as a highly desirable meeting ground.

❏ The region is the site of many more foreign consulates and trade offices than are located here today.

Cultural activities that celebrate our varied ethnic roots will be strengthened and coordinated to make them more accessible to all citizens and to visiting tourists.

International visitors generally will constitute a substantially larger target market for tourism development, exchange programs and academic study.

The region's overall artistic and cultural activities will merit increasing international attention and interaction.

Local media will develop specialties in international coverage that are of a quality meriting national and world syndication.

Cooperation with other parts of the Pacific Northwest and with the Canadian West—the informal but genuine binational region of "Cascadia"—will be a working reality in local and state business and government planning.

Binational regionalism also will become common in the fields of sports, education, the arts, medicine and various nonprofit enterprises.

The community, most importantly, will value and retain its international leadership in aerospace and software, and will emerge as a world leader in such fields as environmental technology, biotechnology, telecommunications, entertainment and consulting services.

If all of these developments were to happen tomorrow, the prospect would be breathtaking: a metropolitan region suddenly achieving maturity even as it reinvigorated its economy and restated its sense of identity. However, change still doesn't come that fast, though great strides have been made in the past 15 or 20 years, The danger is, the change may come so slowly that we don't notice it or plan for it.

Seattle and its close neighbors have done well in the past when they have looked ahead, planned well and acted decisively. Consider our universities, parks, boulevards, water and electric utilities, and ports— all products of determined visionaries at the turn of the century. Also, without similar visionaries a generation ago, we would not have had the varied improvements—in container facilities, park expansions, historic preservation, sewage treatment, health care and bus service—that, in a remarkably quiet fashion, have preserved the area's livability into the present era.

In almost every case, good planning has not only achieved its stated aims, but exceeded them. On the other hand, neglect and drift have given us even worse results than feared. The realms of rapid transportation, regional governance and public education quickly come to mind, although all three are receiving long-overdue attention.

The vision described in this report is wholly practical, so much so that, if enacted, it eventually is likely to be seen as the result of predictable trends. However, while some elements in this picture of metropolitan Seattle in the year 2000 are possibly inevitable, their full benefits are not. The recommendations in the second half of the report will require strong leadership to be implemented. Whether we in this area take real advantage of our opportunities or just assume their fulfillment surely will depend on conscious community action.

2. What Are the Advantages of Global "Citistates"?

Cities of the 21st century, if they hope to prosper, will be truly international communities. The most successful and competitive of them will be closely interconnected to the rest of the world— economically, culturally, technologically, and, to varying degrees, politically. In his new book, author Neal R. Peirce calls them "Citistates." *(See page 6.)*

Already in the 1990s, the most vibrant, thriving urban areas are those that reach out to embrace and welcome the world through trade, tourism, education, services, the arts, sports, media and other means of exchange. They are integral members of what is fast becoming a global society.

Moreover, the key participants in this genuine

"new world order" will not be just the traditional central cities, but entire metropolitan regions that include urban and suburban areas, so-called "edge cities," surrounding towns, and some of the rural areas that encompass them. These regions simply must cooperate and coordinate their efforts more closely to be competitive in the new global economy. Metropolitan regions that ignore or resist this trend will do so at their peril.

The metropolitan Seattle area—from Everett to Tacoma, from Bainbridge Island to the Cascade Mountains—is already a successful international community in many ways. This region—which generally will be referred to in this report as "metropolitan Seattle" although it also includes such major cities as Bellevue, Kirkland, Redmond, Renton, Kent, Issaquah and others, as well as Tacoma and Everett—is the focal point of a state whose international connections are extensive and growing.

Still, in the decade ahead, metropolitan Seattle not only could and should—but, indeed, must—better organize itself to take advantage of its international potential. A clear strategy of continued integration into the new world economy and culture is crucial to this area's future prosperity and global competitiveness. It alone will allow this region to join the recognized leadership communities of the next century—those with a true "international franchise," as some have called it.

More than ever, market exchanges operate in

Defining the Metropolitan Region

Granted, the term "metropolitan Seattle" has some problems. First, there are longtime concerns by other cities in the region about being dominated or overshadowed by Seattle, when they have become in many ways internationally active in their own right.

Second, it is difficult to come up with a precise or official definition of metropolitan Seattle. The U.S. Census Bureau defines the Seattle Primary Metropolitan Statistical Area (PMSA) as King and Snohomish Counties, the Tacoma PMSA as Pierce County, and the Consolidated Metropolitan Statistical Area (CMSA) as all three counties. But "CMSA" is hardly a memorable moniker.

Other terms have problems too. "Greater Seattle," used by the Chamber of Commerce and the Trade Development Alliance, is confined largely to King County. It is also subject to frequent jibes by those who wryly or whimsically promote a mythical "Lesser Seattle." The Municipality of Metropolitan Seattle, or "Metro," which handles the transit and sewer systems, also covers primarily King County, and is now being merged into King County as a result of the 1992 election. The Puget Sound Regional Council (formerly Council of Governments) includes King, Snohomish, Pierce and Kitsap Counties. But the terms "Puget Sound region" or "Central Puget Sound " are awkward and geographically imprecise, and are not widely recognized elsewhere.

Like it or not, most big metropolitan regions are generally known worldwide by the names of their largest central city, although other levels of government clearly have legitimate stakes in the region's identity. Thus, we will use "metropolitan Seattle" in this report and define it as the urbanized areas of King, Pierce and Snohomish Counties, plus Bainbridge Island in Kitsap County. No one has yet suggested a better term, and the Seattle name certainly is the best known in international circles.

constant, real-time, computerized motion. Mergers and buyouts transfer ownership—and a sense of community prosperity—to distant centers. And human capital is only somewhat less mobile than financial capital. This is clearly recognized, even taken for granted, by the most successful international metropolises, such as London, New York, Los Angeles and Tokyo, as well as by some mid-sized cities such as Vancouver, B.C., Atlanta and Amsterdam. Whether consciously and deliberately, or unconsciously and ineffectively, most communities are already an inextricable part of the global marketplace and culture.

A competitive international strategy will become even more important as the European Community gradually transforms itself into the world's largest trading bloc, as the former Soviet Union and the Eastern European nations it long dominated become more independent, as the developing world continues to progress, and as the North American Free Trade Agreement moves toward implementation. At the same time, technology will decree decentralization and dispersal of intellectual power and a closer linkage between the myriad of information-age activities and economic prowess.

To succeed in this environment, moreover, urbanized areas must more effectively market themselves as cohesive regions—not as quarreling collections of separate and independent cities, surrounding suburbs or unincorporated rural areas. Metropolitan cooperation can accomplish much more than parochial competition. In the new global economy, metropolitan regions—even more than states, and perhaps even more than nations—are the key entities that compete in world markets.

The Corporation for Enterprise Development, in its "1992 Development Report Card for the States," flatly declared: "Election-year speeches notwithstanding, there is no U.S. economy. The country is simply too big and too diverse to be characterized as a single economic entity. National economic policy must take into account that our economy is a collection of regional economies with lives of their own—some thriving, some reviving, some weakening, some barely breathing."

Such noted urbanologists as Lewis Mumford, Jane Jacobs and Neal R. Peirce have long argued that metropolises are the true sources of economic energy. In *Cities and the Wealth of Nations* (1984), Jacobs wrote that the failures of national governments to influence economic activity "suggest that nations are essentially irrelevant to promoting economic success," and that of all the various types of economies, "those of cities are unique in their power to shape the economies of other settlements, including ones far removed geographically." Jacobs contended that the true engines of the global economy are what she called "city regions," which are not defined by city, county or state lines, but by the spontaneous boundaries of their regional economies.

More recently, in a 1992 report for the National League of Cities, "The U.S. Common Market of Metropolitan Economies," William R. Barnes and Larry C. Ledebur argue that metropolitan regions are the fundamental building blocks of national economies. Regions transcend geographical and political boundaries because the global economy is so intertwined, they say. Significantly, the NLC has chosen the topic of "Cities and Towns in the Global Economy" for a special seminar at its fall 1993 annual meeting.

And a new book called *Citistates: How Urban America Can Prosper in a Competitive World* (1993), by syndicated columnist and author Neal R. Peirce (with Curtis W. Johnson and John Stuart Hall), argues that the world's great metropolitan areas have become enormously influential bodies. "Inexorably, a metropolitan focus drives one to visualize our great cities, their suburbs, exurbs and geographic realms of influence, as Citistates—critical actors, more 'on their own' in the world economy than anyone would have dreamed since the birth of the Nation State in the 16th and 17th centuries," Peirce writes. "We choose the new word, Citistates, to emphasize the trans-global connectedness, the growing world population domination, of these entities....Across America and across the globe, Citistates are emerging as a critical focus of economic activity, of governance, of social organization for the 1990s and the century to come." Surely that assessment is correct, and metropolitan Seattle must move toward "Citistatehood."

Peirce and his co-authors note that no American

Boeing Cutbacks

For the past two decades, metropolitan Seattle—thanks largely to its extensive international trade activities—seemed relatively exempt from the agonizing economic contractions that have unsettled other parts of the U.S. This region may not have been booming, but it was experiencing at least slow, steady growth. That situation changed dramatically with The Boeing Company's January 1993 announcement of 35 percent production cuts, which will mean the loss of about 20,000 jobs over the next two years. Deliveries of Boeing commercial jets may drop to 340 in 1993, compared to 446 in 1992.

The global recession and accompanying slump in the world airline business, which meant delivery delays or cancellations of new airplane orders, made Boeing's action inevitable. While the cutbacks are not as drastic as those in the late 1960s, when Boeing lost 60 percent of its jobs, they clearly will have a far-reaching impact on the regional economy. Every Boeing job produces about three other jobs, and in King and Snohomish Counties, more than one of every two manufacturing jobs is involved in airplane production.

Overall, the Boeing cuts are likely to mean a flat economy statewide in 1993-94, with employment growth falling to 1 percent or less instead of the 2-3 percent forecast earlier. Still, Boeing's strong balance sheet, high cash reserves, good quality control, and commitment to research and development, should keep its long-term prospects favorable, according to most aerospace industry analysts. Significantly, Boeing's foreign orders remain relatively solid, especially from Russia and Asia, including booming China.

"Citistate" has fully mobilized its community's skills and resources to face the growing challenges of the new world economy. They mention Atlanta's pledge to become an international city and to be chosen as host to the 1996 Summer Olympic Games, Indianapolis's adoption of an amateur sports strategy, and Denver's drive to build a new airport and attract international carriers. "But take the measure of what makes a truly great international Citistate on the world stage—economic cohesiveness, cultural distinction, environmental safety, social equity, livability, physical safety—and most American Citistates lag well behind their European and Asian counterparts," they declare.

Indeed, some urban regions around the world have undertaken conscious efforts to become more competitive international communities. A few, such as Singapore and Hong Kong, have set specific goals, while others, like Amsterdam and Lyons, have designated a specific organization to take the lead in their international efforts. It is not necessary to replicate the specific efforts of such places, but metropolitan Seattle clearly can learn some lessons from them.

An encouraging step in this direction was the European Study Mission, a week-long trip held in April 1992 under the cosponsorship of the City of Seattle, the Greater Seattle Chamber of Commerce and the Trade Development Alliance of Greater Seattle. Seventy Seattle-area civic leaders visited Amsterdam, Rotterdam, and Stuttgart (and briefly, Bonn) to see how these cities are dealing with the challenges of the global economy. The trip's overall theme was "The Competitive Region." Its goal was to address the questions: What does it take to make our urban area globally competitive and how can we best tell the world about ourselves?

In each city visited, the Seattle delegation focused

on such issues as port and airport development, trade and tourism promotion, land-use planning, mass transit and workforce training. The group returned with a long list of ideas and approaches that could be applied here. In the years ahead, this trip will surely be seen as a critical turning point in metropolitan Seattle's evolution as an internationally competitive region. (Planning is already underway for a second international Intercity Visit — to the Kansai region of Japan in the spring of 1994.)

Granted, few of the generally contented residents of metropolitan Seattle want their community to become another Amsterdam, Rotterdam or Stuttgart—much less another New York, Los Angeles or Tokyo. In the past, some people have talked of Seattle becoming a "Geneva of the Pacific" or "another Copenhagen"—a mid-sized international community with special scenic, cultural and civic attractions. However, it would be futile to model ourselves on these very different cities—one a U.N. center, the other a national capital—in any case. Preferably, metropolitan Seattle should simply enhance its best natural and human attributes and seek its own areas of excellence in the international arena.

Achieving a distinct position as an internationally competitive community is desirable for several reasons. Cities that isolate themselves or turn inward will surely stagnate. The world's economy and culture are integrating too quickly for any major metropolitan regions to remain aloof or apart.

Holdouts will quickly find themselves becoming provincial backwaters, with declining employment, falling tax revenues, and the host of social and ecological ills that beset regions of decay.

A strategy of internationalism, especially when combined with high technology, offers the best prospect, paradoxically, of maintaining our most desirable existing regional qualities. It puts a premium on educational excellence, environmental quality and the amenities that make a place attractive and appealing. It brings more variety and vigor to the arts, the media, schools, colleges and universities, and civic organizations. This attracts talented and capable people, who want to come here to visit, study, work and live. Aspiring to the ranks of globally competitive communities actually draws resources—and produces tax revenues—to help make success possible.

Is there a better strategy for this region? Will inertia do more for us? Will negativism—the attitude that all change is for the worse and must be resisted? Could we, for instance, seriously hope to return to full reliance on the commodity and natural resource-centered economy of the last century—trees, fish, and agriculture, important though they are? Could we build any kind of economic security behind a strategy of only heavy manufacturing and retail sales for domestic markets? The international strategy may have problems, but any known alternative has more.

3. Can A Globally Competitive Community Be Defined?

The words "international" and "global," in truth, have so much appeal these days that everyone wants to appropriate them. The business listings section of the Seattle-area telephone book has nearly a full page of companies and organizations whose names begin with the word "International." Dozens of other groups use "Global," "World," "Worldwide" or similar variations.

However, an "international consultant" may turn out to have traveled overseas just a few times and speak a little German or Japanese. A "global enterprise" may merely make occasional overseas telephone calls or send faxes. A "world-famous" restaurant may have postcards on its walls from Rome or Bangkok. And an "international airport" may simply handle prop-jet commuter planes from Canada or Mexico. And the term is surely no guarantee of success: A local firm called "International

Janitorial Services" recently filed for bankruptcy.

Similarly, claims to be an "international city" can be just as inflated and vague. Given the number of cities that refer to themselves as "international," it might be said that the definition is almost what anyone wants it to be. Since any definition inevitably deals with highly subjective values, it is difficult to be too precise, although some individuals and organizations have tried to list key criteria. *(See box below.)*

In the early part of this century, only a handful of cities were generally considered international: London, Paris, Rome, Berlin, Vienna and New York—all world centers of business, government, diplomacy and culture—would have been on anyone's list. Since World War II, such cities as Tokyo, Hong Kong, Los Angeles and Washington, D.C., have joined the first tier, along with a dozen or more other cities that could be listed as well. In the Americas, these probably would include San Francisco, Boston, Chicago, Miami, Montreal, Toronto, Mexico City, and Rio de Janeiro. In Europe: Frankfurt, Munich, Madrid, Amsterdam and Stockholm. In Asia: Singapore, Bangkok, Seoul and Manila.

Indeed, it makes an interesting intellectual exercise—or parlor game—to nominate and evaluate the various contenders. Some cities are internationally renowned in some specialized ways or for unique attractions or events. In the United States, these

Defining an International City

The Institute for the Study of International Cities, headquartered in Montreal, has proposed some objective criteria for defining international communities. Of course, such criteria cannot constitute the last word, but they are valuable guidelines. The institute lists 13 features that define a modern international city:

#1. It is in a geographic position to be open to the world.

#2. It welcomes foreign investment, manpower and services, and engages in foreign trade.

#3. It hosts foreign and international institutions such as corporations, banks, consulates, trade commissions and chambers of commerce.

#4. Its local companies and other institutions have a presence abroad.

#5. It has multiple communication links with other countries.

#6. It is directly linked, through transportation, with other countries.

#7. It has an internationally oriented, advanced service sector— convention halls, exhibition spaces, hotel facilities, international schools, student exchanges, telecommunications networks, etc.

#8. It has mass media with an international presence and reputation.

#9. It has facilities for and welcomes, on a regular basis, international meetings, conventions, festivals, sports events, exhibitions, etc.

#10. Its local or regional institutions, such as universities, museums, and chambers of commerce have an international reputation or impact.

#11. Its public and private institutions have cooperative agreements with international institutions.

#12. Its local government conducts foreign diplomacy and participates in international networks.

#13. Its population has a diverse ethnic make-up and international composition.

(Seattle is among 40 cities in Europe and North America that meet the Institute's criteria.)

would include New Orleans for Mardi Gras, Atlanta for CNN, Orlando for its theme parks, Nashville for country music, Louisville for the Kentucky Derby, Las Vegas for gambling, Honolulu for tourism. Then there are several cities that don't have a particular business or cultural feature for which they are especially known, but are nonetheless international in many ways: Houston, Dallas, San Antonio, San Diego, Baltimore, Philadelphia, Denver, Phoenix, Portland, Minneapolis-St. Paul—and, certainly, Seattle. Elsewhere in North and South America: Vancouver, B.C., San Juan, Sao Paulo and Caracas would fit this category.

Europe has many cities that are well known for a special quality or focus: Geneva as a center of diplomacy, Rotterdam for its vast port, Vienna for its cultural attractions and international meetings, Venice for its canals, museums and festivals, Lyons as a regional center, Milan as a fashion and design leader, Brussels as the seat of the European Community, The Hague for the World Court. A long list of other cities have more general appeal: Copenhagen, Lisbon, Helsinki, Stuttgart, Cologne, Salzburg, Zurich, Barcelona, and Athens. Now that the Iron Curtain is gone, such cities as Moscow, St. Petersburg, Prague, Budapest and Warsaw are becoming increasingly international places for business, culture and exchange programs. In Asia and Asia Minor, Shanghai, Beijing, Delhi, Calcutta, Istanbul, and a few emerging cities (Kuala Lumpur, Jakarta, Islamabad) probably qualify as international cities. So do Sydney, Australia, and perhaps Auckland, New Zealand. In Africa, Cairo, Nairobi, and Johannesburg would be on most lists.

Most of the world's leading international cities, however dissimilar they may be otherwise, often share certain cosmopolitan qualities—healthy trading sectors, a diversity of business interests, a variety of ethnic neighborhoods, an appreciation for the values of different cultures, a wide range of available foods, music, arts, and entertainment, and some unique distinction that is recognized in other countries. The most competitive of these communities are well organized to reach out and welcome international visitors, whether tourists, business people, conference attendees, exchange students, performing artists or others.

Internationally competitive communities fully understand the value of global commerce and promote free and open world trade. They usually offer the highest quality in international services such as banking, accounting, consulting, legal

services, customs brokerages and freight forwarders. Key elements of their trade infrastructure—ports, airports, railroads, highways and other transportation facilities—are the very best that they can provide. They do not fear foreign investment or involvement in their communities, but actively pursue and welcome it.

Many regularly host international conventions, conferences and seminars. They may have major nonprofit organizations, private foundations or think tanks that are active on an international scale. They have world-renowned medical facilities that draw physicians and patients from other countries. Their civic institutions, both public and private, have established formal ties or informal networks with their counterparts in other countries.

International cities try to make sure that their stores, parks, museums, galleries, tours, transit systems and other amenities are convenient and accessible to foreign visitors. They usually have a reputation for being hospitable and courteous to people from throughout the world, regardless of race, creed, color or culture. And they may have a special quality—natural beauty, tourist attraction, unusual festival, historic architecture, communications center, or entertainment district—that is recognized around the world.

Citizens of such communities—in comparison

with others—tend to pay closer attention to international news and world events. They travel more widely and study foreign languages. They attend more international art, music and other cultural events. They enjoy ethnic cooking and restaurants. They usually place a high value on international education for children in elementary and secondary schools, and for students in colleges and universities. They often participate in exchange programs, taking time to live, study or work in other countries—and to host foreign visitors who come to their own cities to do the same. In many ways, they are actively engaged in the rest of the world and keenly aware of global interdependence.

But, as Dr. Panayotis Soldatos, director of the Institute for the Study of International Cities, has said, the list of international criteria is always changing: "To qualify, cities can't sit back. They have to keep moving forward because being international is a dynamic, not a static, phenomenon."

One of the Montreal Institute's efforts is the New International Cities Era (NICE) project, which was begun in the mid-1980s by a group of academics and municipal officials in the United States, Canada and Western Europe. The NICE project focuses on how cities are coping with increasing globalization and how they can protect and improve their interests in an interdependent world economic system. The project has sponsored several conferences and publications, including a book, *The New International Cities Era: The Global Activities of North American Municipal Governments* (1989).

Just how cities rise to the challenge of internationalism is the subject of another book, *Cities in a Global Society* (1989), edited by Richard V. Knight and Gary Gappert. It is a collection of provocative essays on the new phenomenon of global cities. The editors concede that a solid definition of a truly international city—or metropolitan area—does not exist. Still, they argue that as the global economy expands, "Global cities will epitomize global society; they will serve as centers in the multipolar world. Cities that aspire to a role in global society have to define their role and pursue such opportunities aggressively early in the globalization process."

They conclude: "Clearly, many cities, especially those that are national capitals, international financial centers, major ports, industrial centers, or are historic places, have the potential and could be transformed into global cities, but which ones will succeed and thereby sustain their development over the long cycle remains an open question. The process is basically a matter of self-selection, of vision and local initiative."

How Metropolitan Seattle Fares

Does the metropolitan Seattle area fit these varying definitions of an international city? In most ways, yes; in others, no. But in order to be acknowledged as a truly competitive international community, we will have to address the full list one way or another in the years ahead. Some of what this region does in international affairs is remarkable. Some is worth noting, but not really exceptional. And some elements are now being neglected or handled poorly. But there is no question that the potential is there.

Metropolitan Seattle has a strategic location astride a spectacular, protected deep-water harbor. It has exceptional scenic beauty and a comparatively unspoiled environment. If, as a Gallup Poll once reported, people feel happiest when living in sight of mountains or water, then this probably primordial desire can be satisfied as well here, with mountains on two sides and water all around, as anywhere in the world. Vancouver, B.C., rivals this setting, as in slightly different ways do San Francisco, Geneva, Capetown and Rio de Janeiro. But it's still an unusual blessing.

Seattle's easy-going nature and largely peaceful history impose a fairly tolerant mindset and even a kind of temperamental homogeneity, but there is considerable ethnic and racial diversity. Ethnic strife exists, but does not seem high by world standards, and Seattle, within the United States, is considered a comparatively good place to live by most minorities. *(Ebony* magazine once rated it as the best place for African Americans to live.) Seattle is still notable for a relatively fair-minded and involved citizenry. It has excellent, if not world-renowned, museums, opera, symphonies, ballet, theater companies, galleries and other cultural attractions. It has one of the most interesting and attractive public food markets in the world. Its downtown remains vibrant for shopping and sightseeing, now even on Sundays, though its future has been clouded by the recent closure of one premier and one smaller department store. Seattle is widely known as a hospitable city that welcomes visitors, or at least does not mistreat them.

Unquestionably and crucially, the metropolitan Seattle area's economy is already deeply involved and quite competitive in the global marketplace. Seattle's geographical position makes it the closest U.S. mainland port to Asia. Seattle-Tacoma International Airport is nearly equidistant between Tokyo and London. Its premier airplane industry, headed by The Boeing Company, leads the world. And several new high-technology companies here, led by Microsoft, have become household names worldwide.

International trade is the hallmark of internationalism almost anywhere, and its motivating force. Internationalism in other fields, except perhaps tourism or scholarship (consider Florence, Salzburg, Kyoto and Oxford, for example), cannot prosper without strong international trade.

The metropolitan area is the hub of a state that has been for about a decade the most trade-dependent in the nation, with per capita exports—now almost $6,000 per person—that are more than three times the U.S. average. "One in five"—the estimate that international trade supports nearly one out of every five jobs—has become a familiar axiom.

Overall, according to the state Department of Trade and Economic Development, Washington state's two-way international trade increased to more than $74 billion in 1992—more than double the $30 billion of 1980 and a more than five-fold increase over 1977's $13.8 billion mark. That quintupling in trade in only 15 years is an astonishing development by any standard.

What's more, for the past few years the Census Bureau's Foreign Trade Division has also compiled export statistics on a "state of origin" basis—that is, exports manufactured, grown or produced in a state. The latest figures for 1992 are remarkable: Washington state—which, with 4.9 million people,

ranks 18th in population size—now ranks third in total value of state-of-origin exports, at $30.6 billion. We outpaced all the bigger states except California (population, 30 million; exports, $63.1 billion), and Texas (17 million, $47 billion) and surpassed New York (18 million, $29.4 billion).

And equally impressive is the fact that in the five-year period from 1987-91, Washington state's growth rate in state-of-origin exports was a whopping 129 percent, by far the highest of the nation's top five trading states. With less than 2 percent of total U.S. population, this state produces almost 8 percent of total U.S. exports.

Many of the metropolitan region's citizens may not have stopped to reflect upon either the quantitative or qualitative changes that have transformed, and continue to transform, our region. Not only are these changes historically significant— like the Gold Rush of the turn-of-the-century, or Boeing's booming World War II business—but they also are probably unprecedented in our history. Never before has Seattle's foreign trade grown so much so fast—nor has that of other great American cities recently. In truth, to find parallels in our time, one must look to the economic "tigers" of the Far East, such as Singapore, Hong Kong, Seoul, Taipei and Bangkok. Overwhelmingly, then, it is trade that qualifies us as a major international city today.

What Are Metropolitan Seattle's Drawbacks?

For all its advantages, this area lacks many resources and amenities that make for a truly competitive international community. Its international air service is comparatively limited, and has even been declining in very recent years. It is not even a second-ranking center for international finance. Relatively few international banks have offices here. International banking departments actually have downsized in recent years as local bank ownership has moved out of state. (However, some argue this is less significant in the age of high technology, when so many transactions are handled by computers, than it was in the past.)

Metropolitan Seattle—indeed, the state of Washington—lacks any world-famous tourist attractions, museums or major resorts. Its shopping districts, though uncommonly agreeable, are not sufficient by themselves to draw many tourists from outside the region. It does not yet have a state-of-the-art conference center with simultaneous translation capability for international meetings (though it soon will have one).

The Seattle area's media, while they serve local and regional audiences well, are not yet of international renown. Coverage and analysis of international events and affairs, while sometimes excellent, is inconsistent. This is particularly true for coverage of international conferences and meetings on foreign affairs issues held in Seattle. International news generally does not yet carry the weight here that it does in New York, Washington, D.C., Los Angeles, or even (because of CNN), Atlanta. Of course, some other international cities, such as San Francisco, Rotterdam and Bangkok, also lack world-renowned news media.

Metropolitan Seattle's public transportation system is not considered on a par with mass-transit systems in some other international cities, though, again, it is better than many. Metro recently was rated the best large public-transit system in the nation by the American Public Transit Association, which cited the success of the downtown bus tunnel and all-time high ridership on Metro buses. At the same time, the metropolitan area's traffic congestion, partly due to the geography that put downtown Seattle in a narrow stretch with water on both sides, has been ranked the fourth-worst in the United States. Daily "rush hour" periods seem to be getting steadily longer. Taxi service and quality are often erratic.

Street crime is a growing problem despite efforts to deal with it through increased police patrols, private security forces and innovative city ordinances. Homelessness seems an intractable problem, with some downtown sidewalks and parks crowded with "street people"—most of them mentally ill, drug addicts or alcoholics who challenge our capacity to provide humanitarian treatment, let alone permanent and productive jobs. These are "domestic" problems, of course, but it is interesting that visitors from abroad, even while generally praising our area, often mention them. And, although there are no statistics

to prove it, fear of crime undoubtedly deters some potential visitors from coming here.

Metropolitan Seattle also comes to attention for its incompletion, its noble but unfinished schemes. Critics' lists vary, but most would agree, for example, that Seattle Center, location of the "Century 21" World's Fair of 1962, which helped put Seattle on the global map, has become an inadequate, disappointing facility long overdue for renovation. Encouragingly, a $150 million makeover has begun, including renovation of the Coliseum, construction of a new Children's Theater, upgrading of the International Fountain, and plans for a new Jimi Hendrix Museum to showcase Seattle rock music.

Many people believe that the city of Seattle still needs more downtown parks and open space, that the urban core is like an attractive race course with no beginning or end, no sizable place to relax, eat and drink—like Rome's Via Veneto, Copenhagen's Strøget, Paris' Tuilleries, Barcelona's Ramblas, San Francisco's Golden Gate Park, or Vancouver, B.C.'s Stanley Park. An innovative new proposal for creation of a "Seattle Commons" park that would stretch from the northeast end of the shopping district, along Westlake Avenue to South Lake Union, is a reflection of this sentiment. An overall plan for the Commons has been submitted to the City Council, but the scheme still has many obstacles to overcome.

Many residents—and increasingly, many elected leaders—also would like to see more downtown housing, including "affordable" and low-income units. The same contentions are often heard for downtown Tacoma, Bellevue and Everett. The cosmopolitan, bustling international cities of fame usually have considerable numbers of people living near the center, making bustling "life" downtown a constant reality.

Still, despite these evident problems and shortcomings, many local citizens exhibit an attitude of smugness about the region's attributes that is a kind of justifiable local pride but also can be seen as narrow-minded or provincial. It's fine to be proud of your home, but to be overly boosterish—or defensive in the face of criticism—seems a bit silly to international visitors.

Also, although most people believe in a

reasonable balance between environmental preservation and economic progress, this area has a widespread reputation for reflexive resistance to growth and development. There is a perception of greater concern for the environment (often abstract and legalistic) than for the economy, for trees and animals over people and jobs. (See the *Fortune* magazine survey, cited below.) As a result, potential international investors and business people may hesitate to come here for fear of being embroiled in interminable quarrels. If the metropolitan Seattle area is regarded as anti-business, people will simply take their investments, companies, buildings or other projects elsewhere. Without solid economic growth—and therefore government revenue growth—it is hard to see how the environment can be protected, particularly the environment people experience daily: their parks and recreation areas, water and air.

Finally, Washington State is high in per capita tax burden—tenth in the nation in combined state and local taxes, according to the most recent U.S. Census Bureau ranking. This dubious distinction is overlooked by business investors who are impressed by the area's other attractions. As of this writing, that is still true, but—for the future—the area's global competitiveness must be kept in mind when new taxes (or, for that matter, fees, regulations, etc.) are proposed. At a June 1993 conference on technology and economic development, sponsored by U.S. Rep. Jennifer Dunn, R-Bellevue, many of about 200 business leaders present expressed deep concern about this state's tax burden and regulatory system. They noted that entrepreneurs need "carrots, not sticks," and that many of this state's legislators seemed "downright hostile" to business. Our competition is worldwide and government overhead costs are part of what makes for successful sales and investment and jobs—or what helps to discourage them.

4. How Do Others See Us?

A glowing tribute to Seattle as an internationally competitive city came in *Fortune* magazine's Nov. 2, 1992, issue. It ranked Seattle "the best city for global business in the U.S.," based on a nationwide survey of 900 business executives (all *Fortune* subscribers). Seattle ranked highest among 60 American cities. The top 10:

1. Seattle; 2. Houston; 3. San Francisco; 4. Atlanta; 5. New York; 6. Raleigh/Durham; 7. Denver; 8. Chicago; 9. Boston; 10. Orlando.

Fortune somewhat hyperbolically described Seattle as "the cosmopolitan confluence of software and salmon, airframes and apples, where the world's sharpest minds sip rich coffee with the folks who wield sharp axes and fishhooks, in a setting that would make a postcard manufacturer pant. What do you call a town that is home to America's richest entrepreneur and to its biggest exporter, among many other flourishing enterprises; home to one of the country's busiest ports and best state universities; home to some of its most breathtaking vistas (sea, mountain, forest) and smoothest racial relations?"

Fortune based its rankings on a wide range of factors, and noted that no single one determined the outcome. It asked the question: "What makes not just Seattle, but any city, an international city?" Among the qualities *Fortune* listed:

TRANSPORTATION, ESPECIALLY AIR TRANSPORT. International air service is vital to attract international business. But while *Fortune* praised Atlanta's and Denver's airports, it didn't even mention Sea-Tac, merely noting that Seattle "may need more airport capacity."

GRADE A RESEARCH UNIVERSITIES AND MEDICAL CENTERS. These can spin off businesses and anchor technologies that attract global customers, *Fortune* said. It cited the Fred Hutchinson Cancer Research Center as the nation's largest recipient of National Institute of Health grants, adding: "Seattle is bubbling with biotech."

AN INFRASTRUCTURE CAPABLE OF DELIVERING SOPHISTICATED SERVICES, SUCH AS FOREIGN BANKS

THAT OVERSEAS COMPANIES CAN USE. But *Fortune* didn't mention that Seattle's international banking capacity has declined somewhat in recent years as banks consolidate and move their head offices elsewhere.

QUALITY OF LIFE. Attractive natural environment and recreational opportunities ranked high among *Fortune*'s criteria. The magazine emphasized that economic growth helps build quality of life, and vice versa.

In brief descriptions of each city, *Fortune* included some additional criteria:

DAILY INTERNATIONAL FLIGHTS. Seattle was in the 15-24 per day range, the same as Atlanta and Denver, but well below Houston (25-49), San Francisco (50-74) and New York (100 plus).

PERCENTAGE OF SKILLED AND FOREIGN-EMPLOYED WORKERS IN THE LABOR FORCE. Seattle had 47 percent skilled workers, more than any other cities in the top 10 except Raleigh/Durham (49.2 percent) and Boston (49 percent). However, Seattle's percentage of workers employed by foreign-owned companies, 4.9 percent, was among the lowest in the top 10; only Orlando (4.6 percent) and Denver (4.2 percent) were lower.

MANUFACTURING COMPETITIVENESS INDEX. This was one of two new indices *Fortune* developed for its 1992 survey. It reflects changes in manufacturing employment, wages, exports, value added per worker, and high-tech employment in each city. Seattle's

Washingtonians' Views on International Trade

Most Washington residents are aware of the important role that international trade plays in this state, according to a survey by Elway Research. Of 387 residents polled statewide, 40 percent said their jobs were "entirely," "somewhat," or "indirectly" dependent on foreign trade—although 41 percent called their jobs "not at all" trade dependent. Most Washingtonians were aware of the North American Free Trade Agreement (NAFTA), and by a 2-to-1 margin respondents said they expected its impact to be good for this region, because it will open borders for more trade, stimulate the economy and create jobs.

Overall, the survey found residents well-educated on trade issues, contrary to assertions that people are not appreciative of the role trade plays in the state's economy. The survey found that despite the unfavorable U.S.-Japan trade balance, respondents by a 2-to-1 ratio thought trade with Japan does "more good than harm" to this state. On the other hand, 64 percent felt that foreign investment in Washington real estate did "more harm" than good, and 53

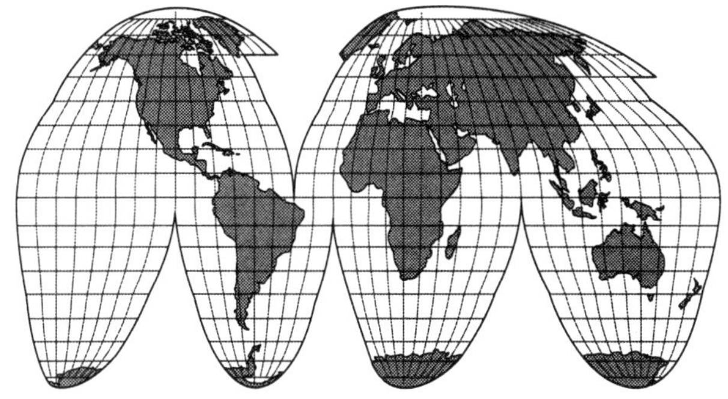

percent felt the same way about purchase and construction of factories here by foreign companies. Also, a 41 percent plurality statewide believed that Japanese purchase of the Seattle Mariners did "more harm" than good—although that figure would no doubt be much different in the Seattle metropolitan area. And on the plus side, 67 percent of respondents said that sending state officials on trade missions to other countries did "more good," and 56 percent said the same about cooperation between Boeing and Japan to build aircraft.

(SOURCES: The Elway Poll; *Seattle Post-Intelligencer*, Dec. 4, 1992)

score of 114 (100 was the average) was higher than any city on the top 10 except Raleigh/Durham (138) and Orlando (124).

INTERNATIONAL PRESENCE INDEX. This category reflects the number of foreign banks, consulates and service firms, plus employment by foreign-owned companies, regarded as a leading indicator of foreign investment. Seattle's score was 100, lower than any cities in the top 10 except Raleigh/Durham, Denver and Orlando.

PRO-BUSINESS ATTITUDE. Of *Fortune*'s 60 cities, Seattle ranked in the bottom half (34th) in terms of its supportive attitude toward business. Noting the state's growth-management legislation, "Lesser Seattle," and the city's "urban villages" plan, the magazine conceded, "the place still doesn't quite embrace development." It quoted Immunex CEO Steve Duzan on how it took his company 4 1/2 months to get a permit to install an air conditioner, and Boeing Chairman Frank Shrontz on how his firm had to spend an extra $50 million for environmental and other mitigation costs on its new 777 plant in Everett.

Fortune's blessing was clearly a coup for Seattle, and the article will be a valuable promotional tool. But it's well to remember that this city still has some shortcomings as an international competitor. Interestingly, a followup survey of local leaders in December 1992 found many people here somewhat skeptical—or perhaps merely more realistic—about *Fortune*'s ranking of Seattle as the best city for global business in the U.S.

The survey was conducted by The Economic Development Council of Seattle & King County at a meeting with *Fortune* representatives. Of 116 responses, only 42 percent said their local communities were properly organized to satisfactorily support international trade and commerce, while 44 percent felt their communities were not so organized.

Moreover, while nearly 100 percent of respondents rated the Puget Sound region's airport, banking services, harbor facilities, legal services, hotels and restaurants as "excellent" or "good," people were sharply critical of other shortcomings in this region's ability to remain competitive in the global economy. Taxes and transportation were major concerns. Sixty-

A Few Recent Rankings

The last few years have seen Seattle ranked highly in a number of listings by various organizations and publications. A few examples, as compiled by the Seattle-King County Convention and Visitors Bureau:

❏ A 1990 reader's choice poll in *Conde Nast Traveler* magazine ranked Seattle the No. 8 favorite city in the world to visit; the city ranked No. 10 in the magazine's 1989 poll.

❏ *Money* magazine in 1993 ranked Seattle the 11th-most-livable city in the U.S., down from No. 2 in 1990 and No. 1 in 1989.

❏ Bicycling magazine in 1990 named Seattle the Best North American City for Bicycling.

❏ A Louis Harris survey (1989) named Seattle the No. 2 best place in the U.S. to locate a business.

❏ USA Today (1989) named Seattle the No. 1 City of the Future.

❏ The Zagat Hotel Survey in 1989 said Seattle had the Best Hotels in the United States; of 4,000 frequent travelers who participated in the independent survey, Seattle outranked all other U.S. cities in hotel quality, service and dining.

Metropolitan Seattle's "User-Friendliness"

A survey entitled "Is Seattle 'User Friendly' to International Visitors?" was conducted in the fall of 1992 by Elway Research Inc. for the Trade Development Alliance of Greater Seattle, with the help of a grant from Goldman Sachs. The goal was to gather information from those who regularly host international visitors and guests.

Questionnaires were mailed to foreign-owned companies, Sister City committees, consulates, international chambers of commerce, non-profit groups and others. Of 350 questionnaires sent, 72 were completed, for a return rate of 21 percent (which is above average for a direct mail survey).

In general, survey results were positive. This region was considered sensitive to international visitors, especially in our hotels and shopping areas. Respondents gave Seattle good marks for its hospitality and "ease of use." Overall, the city's grade was a "A" to "B" with 87 percent rating Seattle's hospitality as "excellent" (46 percent) or "good" (41 percent). In addition, 74 percent said it was "easy for an international guest to function in Seattle," but only 12 percent called it "very easy." Asked to name the "best things about Seattle," respondents cited its friendliness and openness to international guests, its natural beauty, and its cleanliness.

Suggested improvements included more information and materials available in languages other than English, public transportation systems, improvements in the Immigration and Naturalization Service offices, and more convenient banking services. Greater Seattle's highest ratings were for shopping (80 percent called it "excellent" or "good"). The lowest ratings were for taxi service (62 percent rated it only "fair" or "poor.")

However, there are some reasons to be cautious about the survey results. Since most of the respondents were not themselves international guests or visitors, they were reporting primarily on what they had heard—and negative comments may be more likely to be expressed than positive ones. At the same time, a preponderance of the respondents were Asian, and in many Asian cultures it is considered impolite to criticize one's host—so negative ratings actually could be understated.

Of the respondents, 46 percent were permanently doing business in Seattle, 15 percent were residents, and 12 percent were diplomats. One in five had lived here more than 20 years and one in five had lived here two years or less. More than a third were Japanese (36 percent), 29 percent were Americans, 10 percent Germans, and 6 percent Koreans.

In summarizing the survey, Elway concluded: "The overall ratings are good, but there is room for improvement. These findings indicate that the attributes Seattlites are most proud of—shopping, natural beauty, friendliness—are the same things that appeal to international visitors. The data also indicate that Seattle has not gone out of its way to make the city accessible and truly 'user friendly.' About one-third to one-half of these respondents rated almost all of these services as only 'fair.'"

The Trade Development Alliance is considering several steps in response to the survey, including: Publishing a new guide on how to "use" the Greater Seattle region, available in several languages; establishing a centrally located kiosk, preferably around Westlake Center, to provide information and services to international visitors; conducting a followup survey of selected companies, and soliciting more information from the Consular Corps and hotel concierges.

(SOURCES: Elway Research, Inc.; Trade Development Alliance of Greater Seattle; *Washington CEO* magazine, January 1993 issue.)

two percent cited business taxes as "poor" or "unacceptable," 60 percent rated the region's roads in the same categories, and 46 percent said the same about public transit.

Even so, concluded Vic Ericson, EDC president: "Local community leaders have a great deal of confidence in our ability to compete globally. There seems to be a general consensus that Seattle is positioning itself as an international center for trade and commerce."

A survey released in June 1992 by the International Association of Corporate Real Estate Executives, which is made up of top facilities planners for major companies, also revealed that many of them look on metropolitan Seattle less favorably than they did in the past. The main concern is the rise in anti-growth activism here, which leads to development fees, permit difficulties and other problems that give pause to business executives looking for new sites. (High lease rates were also cited in the survey: Seattle office space costs as much as $20 a square foot, compared to $4.50 in Dallas.) On the other hand, the Association of Foreign Investors in U.S. Real Estate, in a fall 1992 survey, ranked Seattle the fourth-*best* city for future real-estate investment (behind Washington, D.C., Atlanta and San Francisco).

There seems to be a difference between how metropolitan Seattle is seen in the U.S., where it is relatively well known, and in the international arena, where it generally is not. Among those citizens of other countries who have visited or lived here, feelings are generally positive. For many others, metropolitan Seattle is simply not familiar. Its image is vague, characterized by such comments as: "It rains a lot." "It's nice in the summer." "Boeing controls the economy." "It's supposed to be a livable city." And those truths and half-truths are about all many people know, if they have heard of the area at all.

Discovery Institute hosted a luncheon for members of the Seattle Consular Corps to solicit their impressions, ideas and suggestions on metropolitan Seattle's status as an international community. This was an informal discussion, not a scientific survey, but their opinions were insightful and instructive. (Since we stipulated that the conversation was off the record to encourage candor,

no one will be quoted by name in this report.)

In both Asia and Europe, the consuls agreed, Seattle is not nearly as well known among the general public as, say, Vancouver, B.C., or San Francisco. However, most said that metropolitan Seattle is reasonably well known among people involved in government or trade, especially, of course, the aerospace industry. Interestingly, all pointed out that Seattle is considered a very desirable post for members of their respective foreign services, since it is a livable, friendly city with many environmental and cultural amenities. It was somewhat difficult, in fact, to get the diplomats to express any criticism of metropolitan Seattle. They were careful to couch their observations in a constructive light, not claiming any superiority for their own countries or cities. Answering our request for suggestions for improvements, one consul asked, "Aren't you trying to gild the lily?"

Even so, several consuls—diplomatically, of course—raised some interesting and valid concerns about metropolitan Seattle. For example:

INEFFECTIVE OR COMPETING ORGANIZATIONS. Some said that the metropolitan Seattle area seemed to have too many groups engaged in international activities, often in a half-hearted fashion, and many with competing programs or with overly ideological agendas.

EDUCATIONAL DETERIORATION. Most believed that school systems in this area needed basic reform. Potential foreign investors worry that we are not keeping up in terms of educating students or the workforce, and that this will limit our otherwise excellent prospects for global competitiveness.

POOR PLANNING. It was noted that the metropolitan Seattle area's long-range planning and coordination among various governmental jurisdictions was inadequate compared to major cities in Europe and Asia. (This, of course, is a major theme of our own report.)

TOURIST ATTRACTIONS LIMITED. Several consuls felt that metropolitan Seattle lacks world-class attractions—shopping, resorts, sights—that would draw large numbers of tourists as their primary destination. However, they suggested that this area should better define its attractions—scenic beauty, lack of crowds, friendly populace, etc.—in order to attract more discriminating tourists, especially younger people.

INADEQUATE PROMOTIONAL EFFORTS. Several consuls said that the metropolitan Seattle area needed to promote itself better in world markets, both for trade and tourism.

Finally, it was noted by several consuls that Seattle was somewhat schizophrenic about its aspirations, image and place in the world. "This is a city that is very unsure about what it is," said one. "Many people here don't see the need for more outsiders. Some people aren't at all sure they want to be a more international city." That insight sums up a reality that, in one way or another, will have to be faced. In the end, many residents of this area want the perceived benefits of internationalism without the potential problems.

5. What Issues Does Internationalism Raise?

Not everyone agrees that to become a more competitive international community is a desirable goal. Some critics focus on perceived disadvantages rather than potential advantages. Let's examine some of these arguments.

Economy

Internationalism will only benefit upper-income citizens, one argument goes. The rich will get richer, the poor poorer, and the middle class will stagnate. The benefits of international trade, education and culture won't reach those most in need, this argument continues. Shouldn't we instead use our limited resources to help the homeless, the elderly, drug and alcohol addicts, school dropouts and other disadvantaged people?

The answer is that without a healthy overall economy, we won't be able to help anyone in need— and international activity is one of the best ways to keep our economy healthy. Otherwise, there won't be enough tax revenues to support human services, educational, environmental, or other vital programs. Success in the international arena generates the extra resources a region needs to address social problems. Had we not succeeded as we did in trade over the past decade, our social and governmental problems— starved of the revenue and jobs international trade provided—would have been far worse.

Washington state revenues grew by 46 percent between 1987 and 1991, thanks in great measure to international trade. The current state budget woes,

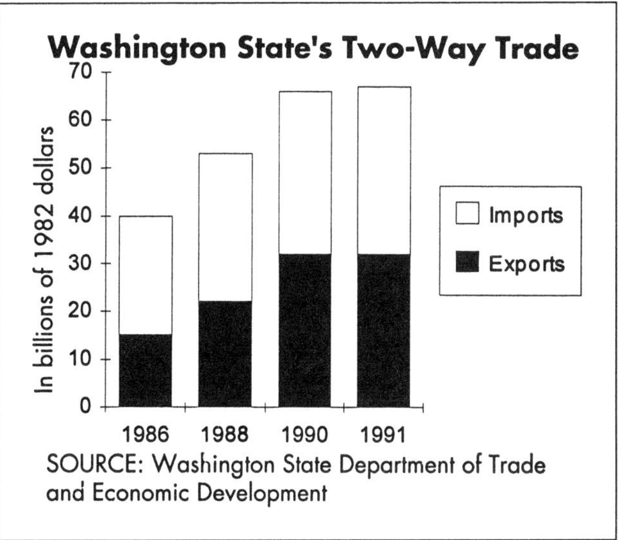

which have led to fierce recriminations in (and out of) state government, would surely be worse had we not been so strong in trade. Funding for all manner of state-financed programs would have been restricted. Unless we continue to increase our trade, the poor, along with taxpayers, will suffer.

National economic statistics bolster this argument: In 1990, some 80 percent of America's economic growth was due to international trade. Every $1 billion in U.S. exports translates into roughly 20,000 jobs for American workers, according to federal Commerce Department estimates.

These facts undermine the argument that internationalism benefits only an elite few. In Atlanta, where some Seattleites raised the "elitist" concern during an intercity visit organized by the Greater

Seattle Chamber of Commerce in 1991, former Mayor Andrew Young responded: "As the market gets bigger, everybody gets a little more." George Berry, former director of Atlanta's Hartsfield International Airport, added that international commerce "puts bicycles under Christmas trees" and said the end result is that more people are leading a better life. Atlanta has a much poorer population than does our area, but sees its international strategy as the best way to help that population.

Growth

Other critics argue that internationalism will only exacerbate our region's growth problems. We shouldn't encourage more international companies to come here, establish offices, build plants or invest funds, because that will mean more sprawl, heavier traffic, greater overcrowding, and environmental degradation. Nor should we encourage tourism or in-migration, which only crowd our favorite attractions and make it harder for local residents to enjoy living here. These critics contend: "We have enough people here already. Let's keep things as they are."

However, even the most zealous of these critics will concede that some growth is simply inevitable. Actually, at least half of this region's population growth is attributable to our own children and their children. We can't prevent growth unless we sharply reduce our birth rate (which is unlikely), erect a wall (which is unconstitutional) or experience a steep economic downturn (which is definitely achievable, but undesirable). Internationalism will help encourage quality growth.

Clean industries, businesses and services are good for everyone in the region. Software, biotechnology, electronics, aerospace, medicine, environmental equipment, marine technology and other growing fields tend to attract well-educated, highly paid workers who pay substantial taxes and don't demand extensive social services. We should emphasize such low-polluting, intellectually oriented growth. Witness the upheavals that have occurred in the timber and fishing industries in recent years.

Tourism

Let's face it: Few local residents anywhere in the

world regard tourists as an unmixed blessing. Consider some of the common complaints about tourists: They overcrowd places, increase traffic congestion, wear silly clothes, gawk too much, ask too many questions, are too demanding, and can't even follow simple directions. Granted, many tourists

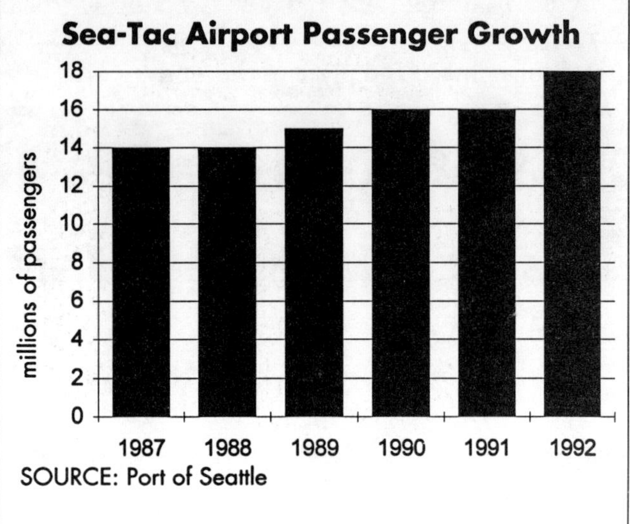

truly are like that. Indeed, so are *we* when we are tourists in someone else's city—especially a foreign city. Travel is unsettling as well as exciting, and it brings out the worst as well as the best in all of us tourists.

However, tourists also flatter us with their praise, they stimulate our thinking, and they seldom commit crimes. Most of all, catering to their needs provides a good, clean industry with relatively low costs. It helps stimulate the local economy through jobs in the hospitality industry—hotels, stores, restaurants, theaters, sports arenas, etc. These often are jobs that wouldn't otherwise exist, and summer or seasonal jobs that are ideal for students. Tourism also helps provide entrepreneurial opportunities for those who want to start guest houses, crafts shops, tour services, rafting companies or other specialized businesses. The same can be said for more international conferences and meetings, which often bring delegates back on return trips as tourists, accompanied by family or friends. Some visitors return as investors.

Immigration

But what if they want to move here? Some critics contend that encouraging more international trade, tourism and exchange programs will lead to more immigration, which might have negative consequences. Too many poor immigrants from Asia, Latin America and Europe are coming here already, they say, demanding a high level of social services,

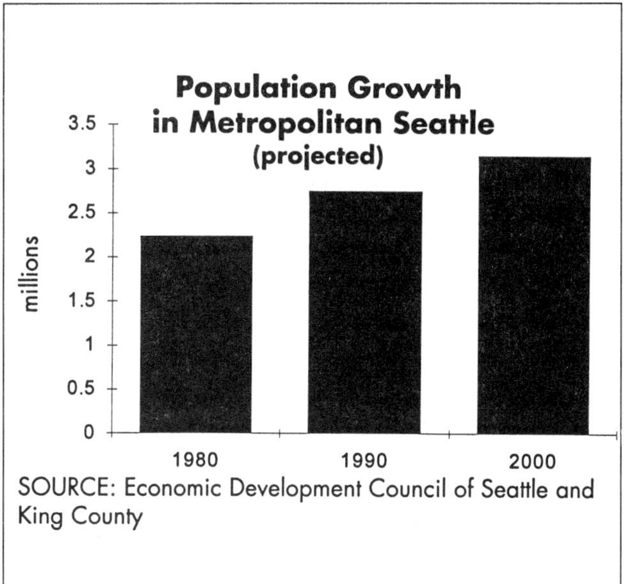

SOURCE: Economic Development Council of Seattle and King County

burdening other taxpayers, and increasing crime, drug, and housing problems. In the schools, they charge, immigrant children need language instruction and other special help, which raises costs and causes cultural problems. Therefore, these critics might conclude, we shouldn't do anything to attract more immigration, which can only lead to cultural alienation among longtime residents.

However, legal immigrants add far more to our economy than they cost us in services of any kind. As a practical matter, immigrants are among the most hard-working, highly motivated members of our community. They start new businesses, put in extra hours of work, and become more productive—and, ultimately, often even more patriotic—than many longtime Americans. Most immigrants become independent and successful as quickly as possible. Moreover, some anti-immigrant attitudes are evidence of outright racism or simple xenophobia, and must be resisted as such.

If we pride ourselves on our openness, tolerance and diversity, as many citizens of the region do, immigrants clearly contribute greatly to helping build a genuine and benign multi-cultural society. In the schools, immigrant children are often among the top academic achievers, and provide a rich mix of cultural heritage that can greatly add to all of our children's education. There surely are sound reasons to prevent illegal immigration, especially the felonious, inhuman smuggling trade. But on balance, legal immigrants pay their way—and they help pay ours.

Resources

Critics also might say that internationalism means exporting more valuable Washington state natural resources—logs, fish, wheat, etc.—without adding enough value. Instead, they insist, we should concentrate on processing more resource products here to provide better, higher-paying jobs for local workers, and resist becoming a "resource colony" of Japan or other countries that make valuable products from our raw materials.

This argument is a good one—up to a point. Although this state's traditional resource-based industries have suffered declines in recent years, they are still an important segment of the economy. Log exports already have been greatly reduced through federal and state restrictions. The forest-products industry is processing an increasing share of timber into lumber, paper and other wood products for export. As for agricultural resources, they are renewable and highly valued worldwide. Washington exports about 35 percent of its total agricultural production, including wheat, apples, fish, cherries, pears and other raw and processed foods. Between 85 and 95 percent of the wheat grown in this state is exported. We should be able to derive full value from selling our agricultural crops and related products to those willing to pay a premium for quality.

Overly restricting the export market and government over-regulation can have unintended side effects and negative consequences, such as discouraging investment, pushing up housing costs, driving away jobs, depressing the economy, and increasing social-services costs.

Conclusion

A strategy of international competitiveness, in the last analysis, surmounts most criticism because it operates in harmony with this region's strengths and needs, in the following ways:

❏ It will mean more high-skilled, high-paying jobs for current residents of this area and their families.

❏ It will provide enough low-skilled jobs to meet the current needs of our regional workforce, but not enough to make the area a magnet for excess unskilled labor from elsewhere.

❏ It complements and abets our existing strength in the high-technology field.

❏ It pays the best return for dollars invested and political effort expended.

❏ And most importantly, it comports with the way the world is headed anyway.

Perhaps there are stronger arguments than we've posed here that could be raised against a strategy of internationalism. But again, it must be stated that any criticisms, to be credible, must offer alternatives. And what might the alternative strategies be? An extraction-based, natural resources economy based on timber and fish simply isn't sufficient anymore, given market, environmental and political realities. A heavy-manufacturing economy based on cheap labor is inconceivable in this region.

Given our geography, there's little chance of becoming a national transportation hub, like Chicago, Denver or Atlanta. A negative "green" strategy of hampering even careful growth, artificially limiting population, and relying solely on small-scale industries has its appeal, but as an overall strategy it has never worked in a modern society anywhere, and really does run the risk of unhealthy elitism.

The most menacing alternative, however, is one of simple indifference and drift, in which our political and business leaders refuse to make decisions or exercise leadership. If we just muddle along, opportunities will be seized by other cities and metropolitan regions that are more focused and assertive. Our own children won't have sufficient job opportunities, or they'll be outclassed by well-trained job-seekers from other areas. We could easily become a stagnant West Coast version of one of the older Rust Belt urban regions. The consequence of failure to define and seize our own future is not to preserve the present indefinitely, but to decay and lose the ability to save or improve what we most value—our environment, schools, industry, arts and other irreplaceable assets, including the most precious: our human capital.

A comprehensive strategy of international competitiveness is the best course for this metropolitan region to pursue in the next decade and beyond. It is not an exclusive strategy, of course. In fact, it is the strategy that will work best with others. It fits not only our regional emphasis on high technology, but also accommodates well to prudent strategies of natural resource management, environmental protection, high-quality urban design and thoughtful social policies. It is an overall strategy for excellence. With such a strategy we will fly with the wind currents rather than against them.

Part II

Recommendations —A Strategy for a More Globally Competitive Community

10 Priority Steps to Create A More Globally Competitive Community

In the first section of this report, we described the rationale for a metropolitan economic strategy based on internationalism—that is, one designed to make a community more globally competitive. We suggested that effective pursuit of this strategy requires involvement of the area's several levels and kinds of government, in addition to business, labor and nonprofit organizations. We drew on hundreds of interviews in the metropolitan Seattle area and on research from a dozen other cities in North America, Europe and Asia. We argued that internationalism should be reflected in overall civic leadership, educational institutions, the arts, environmental and other activities in the region, as well as in the essential realms of manufacturing and trade.

Political and civic leadership is crucial. If metropolitan economies are now recognized (in addition to nations) as fundamental building blocks in the new global economy, and if an international orientation is becoming characteristic of successful metropolitan economies, then one thing is clear: Public officials and other community leaders need to expand their definition of "local" responsibility to include support for the metropolitan area's international strategy. As a matter of practical statesmanship, they also will have to agree to share political turf. This is true of Seattle today and will become true of most metropolitan regions before long.

In the following recommendations we attempt to describe the main elements of a strategy for making metropolitan Seattle a more competitive global community. This strategy is neither trivial nor grandiose; we are not proposing mere "coordination," on one hand, or a new level of government on the other. Rather, the international strategy we propose is increasingly a realistic reflection of our area's interests and opportunities.

Most importantly, we attempt to indicate how the many institutions, groups and individuals in our community can come together to delineate and implement that strategy. The metropolitan area does not lack for diversity. It does tend to lack focus. To provide the focus will take something like a consensus, which brings us back to the issue of leadership.

Leadership

1. RECOMMENDATION: Metropolitan Seattle needs a unified structure for addressing the international concerns that the many sectors of our community have in common. One organization, drawing on the collaborative contributions of all affected levels of government and private groups, should be designated to act as a kind of combined trade and foreign office.

Currently, dealing with the broad range of international affairs as they affect our metropolitan area is a secondary mandate for several federal, state and local governmental bodies, but the primary role of none. The same is true for private-sector groups. For example, when the Philippines recently announced plans to remove its consulate in Seattle, there was no logical, recognized office or organization to make an effort to persuade the Filipinos to reconsider. Similarly, when it became clear that Hungary might be willing to open at least an honorary consulate here—

the first from Eastern Europe—there was no group with clear responsibility to pursue the matter, which therefore became the subject of ad hoc and haphazard arrangements. (Since, however, successful!)

At one time the problem of international concerns falling through the cracks of existing organizations was worse. It was a breakthrough in 1990 when community-wide response to international

The benefits of having a metropolitan Seattle foreign office will make the political risk-taking worthwhile.

concerns led to the creation of the Trade Development Alliance of Greater Seattle. The "TDA" pulled together resources from the City of Seattle, King County, the Port of Seattle, the Greater Seattle Chamber of Commerce and organized labor, with a stated goal of making this region "one of North America's premier international gateways and commercial centers." This public-private model of shared costs and efforts, which is fairly common in Europe and Japan, was unique in the United States at the time; it has since been emulated by other cities and is under study elsewhere. But several elements concerned for the well-being of the metropolitan area are not yet directly involved, nor is the Trade Alliance set up to deal in a clear-cut fashion with non-trade issues.

What is needed now is an organization with 1) a wider geographical range than is present under the Trade Development Alliance, embracing the three or four-county area that is the true metropolitan region; 2) a wider variety of participants, including, for example, higher education, K-12 common schools, and private nonprofit groups involved in foreign affairs; and 3) a wider mandate, extending from trade to the overall strategy for a globally competitive community.

It is likely that the best option for creating such an organization would be to adapt the present Trade Development Alliance to this larger, more inclusive mission. That cannot happen easily, of course. Any one of the three forms of expansion (geographical representation, variety of participants, and mandate) probably will require extensive deliberation and negotiation. The melding of public roles is not easy at any time. It may be politically necessary to do this particular job in steps.

But the benefits of having a metropolitan Seattle foreign office will make the political risk-taking worthwhile. Like a foreign ministry in a country, to borrow another image, the office would give a single focus to our area's many international groups and activities, discussing in one arena the international concerns brought to it by our congressional delegation, state officials, county governments, municipalities, ports, school districts, higher education, business and trade associations, labor organizations, nonprofit and civic groups. The office in turn could provide expert international staff assistance and advice to participating partners. The office would embrace in local scale what is covered nationally, for example, by the International Trade Administration and the office of international tourism at the Commerce Department, and by several offices, including "public diplomacy," at the State Department.

In the short- to mid-term, the office also would be a suitable forum to consider the other recommendations in this report and to help participating levels of government and private groups decide which recommendations they each could commit to implement as part of an overall competitiveness strategy. However, the coordinating function would be just that, not a statutory or policy-enforcement mandate. It would support, and not supplant, activities by specialized groups such as the Japan America Society, Washington Council on International Trade, the World Affairs Council, and the World Trade Club.

We think that metropolitan (and state and federal) leadership is ready for such a function. The 1992 European Study Mission, co-sponsored by the City, the Chamber and the Trade Alliance, was an example of such an emerging public-private partnership. And it helped inspire the Puget Sound Regional Council's current effort to devise a regional economic development strategy—led by Seattle City Councilmember Jim Street (past president of the Regional Council) and Chamber of Commerce Chairman George Walker (chairman of U S WEST). This is an admirable step in the right direction, although it does not concentrate on international competitiveness *per se*. The current effort to create a Cascadia Corridor Commission is another noteworthy example along these lines (see below).

In the first draft of this report, we recommended that representatives of all the levels of government, including education and ports, and the leading business, labor and nonprofit groups, should be called together in an "International Summit," as has been suggested by Seattle Mayor Norm Rice, among others. However, further reflection and discussion has persuaded us that a large gathering is not necessary at this time. Instead, a series of smaller meetings including those interested in helping decide where such a coordinating function will reside and what its mandate should be now seems most appropriate. Indeed, in some ways the Trade Development Alliance is now moving in the direction recommended here; increased contacts with the University of Washington and regional community colleges are a prime example. Still, further progress is needed. If this recommendation is fully implemented, metropolitan Seattle will once more have pioneered an important new approach to urban life: a practical and energetic way to fulfill the vision of a globally competitive community.

Cascadia

> 2. RECOMMENDATION: Metropolitan Seattle's strategy for global competitiveness should embrace a closer alliance with our northern neighbor, Vancouver, B.C., as part of an overall advancement of the binational region of "Cascadia."

The increasing cross-border cooperation in the Pacific Northwest and Canada is one of the most exciting and promising developments in international regionalism in decades. The Seattle/Vancouver tie is crucial. There are few more natural international metropolitan relationships in the world today. Vienna and Budapest? Hong Kong and Guangzhou? Buenos Aires and Montevideo? The list of truly friendly, closely linked international cities is very short.

However, the Seattle/Vancouver connection also must open to include Portland, Ore., as part of the "Cascadia Corridor," a line of interests along the Interstate 5 freeway, and then (still wider) of the whole Northwest U.S. and Western Canada, the land of mountains and water that many have begun to call "Cascadia."

This region also has been referred to as the New

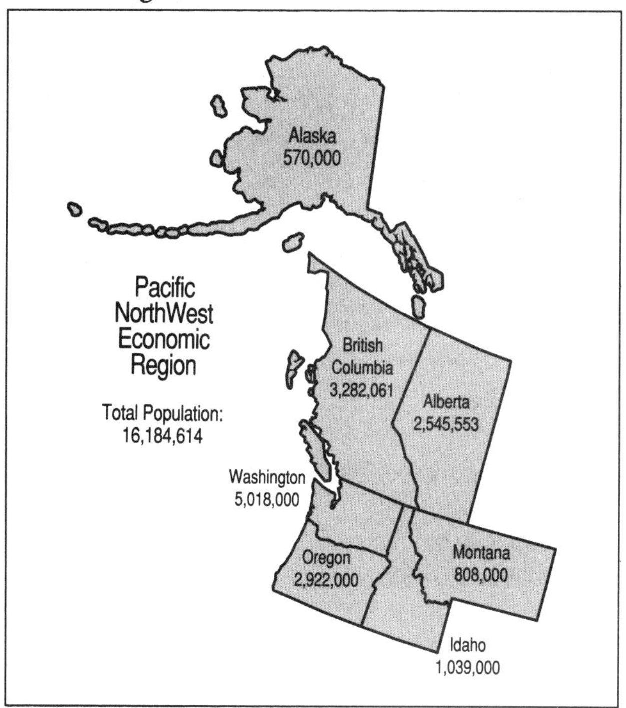

Pacific, the Pacific Northeast, and Ecotopia, but there's no reason to be held back by names. The most important thing is to encourage closer ties between the multi-state, multi-provincial region that includes Washington, Oregon, Idaho, western Montana, British Columbia and Alberta, and possibly Alaska, the Yukon and Northwest Territories as well. This is the binational regional setting for our own internationally minded metropolis. It is potentially advantageous for all who share it as cooperative neighbors. Depending on how the boundaries are defined, Cascadia has an economy greater than all but nine nations in the world. It has more than 16 million inhabitants, with a gross domestic product of about $250 billion a year.

Our state government clearly has a vital role to play in this larger region. And cooperation has been growing for the last several years. During Expo '86 in Vancouver, B.C., Washington state government and business officials began a series of meetings with their Canadian counterparts to discuss common interests. This led to an agreement for formal cooperation between the state and province, and the creation of a 14-member bilateral committee. The name "Pacific Northwest Economic Partnership" was first used by a group of Washington and British Columbian computer companies that worked together at the COMDEX trade show in Las Vegas in November 1988. After the U.S.-Canadian Free Trade Agreement took effect on Jan. 1, 1989, the state of Washington and British Columbia signed two agreements committing themselves to cooperation in areas of mutual economic benefit, especially trade, investment and tourism. Five industries—biotechnology, aquaculture, fashion, marine instruments, and aerospace—were identified for cooperative efforts. Software, information sharing, and environmental engineering technology were added later.

While the Partnership has been primarily an executive branch initiative, the Pacific NorthWest Economic Region (PNWER), has been led by legislative officials. It also has made great progress in a short time, encouraging legislators in the Northwest states and Canada's Western provinces to collaborate in such areas as pollution-control technology, telecommunications linkages, and uniform product content standards. The various legislative bodies already have passed a number of identical bills that will make trade and cooperation much easier. But PNWER operates on a small budget, with staff assistance from the Northwest Policy Center at the University of Washington.

In another major cross-border initiative by the state, an Environmental Cooperation Agreement between Washington and British Columbia was signed by then-Gov. Booth Gardner and Premier Mike Harcourt in May 1992. It may become the basis for a broader "Georgia Straits/Puget Basin Initiative" that would examine how to establish sustainable urban development across municipal, provincial and national boundaries and jurisdictions.

Blaine Peace Arch, U.S.-Canadian border

That reflects a theme of the so-called "Vancouver Declaration," adopted in March 1992 at "Globe '92," which combined a Global Parliamentarians conference on human settlements with an environmental trade show.

There have also been encouraging developments in the private sector. The Pacific Corridor Enterprise Council (PACE), was formed in 1990 by a group of private companies in the region to seek to lower barriers to cross-border trade and commerce in the light of the U.S.-Canada Free Trade Agreement.

More recently, the promising concept of a "Cascadia Corridor Commission" has been advanced to bring together government officials along the Interstate 5 corridor from Vancouver, B.C. to Portland-Eugene, Ore., in a new binational organization. Legislation to provide a $400,000 grant to support the Commission passed Congress. Former Congressman John Miller now leads a Discovery Institute project to make the Commission an effective entity. The Commission's mandate will be to develop a long-term strategic plan for sustainable development in the region, focusing on environmental, transportation, trade, tourism and technology issues. A memorandum of understanding signed by the chief executives of British Columbia, Washington and Oregon is required to inaugurate the commission.

Paul Schell, a Port of Seattle Commissioner who was recently named Dean of the University of Washington's College of Architecture and Urban Planning, has been another longtime proponent of Cascadia. In a speech to the North American Institute, Schell reiterated some ideas that could help. One is bulldozing the checkpoints between the U.S. and Canada, or at least taking steps to make passage much faster and easier. Border crossings at Blaine, Washington, have more than doubled in a decade, from 5 million to 11 million a year—and they are predicted to reach 28 million annually by the year 2000. One step in the right direction was the creation in 1991 of the Peace Arch Crossing Entry (PACE) program, which provides a car decal for frequent travelers that allows them to bypass regular inspection lanes during specified hours. Low-risk travelers with no criminal history or customs or immigration violations are eligible for the PACE decals. By the fall of 1992, Canadian officials reported approving 27,500 decals, while U.S. officials had approved 19,000 applications. This program should be more widely promoted and expanded, eventually leading to even more open borders between the U.S. and Canada.

Another promising project now underway by Discovery Institute and the Cascadia Education Society of Vancouver, B.C., is to develop a marketing program to expand international tourism in Cascadia. This effort would describe the international tourism marketplace and its potential for Cascadia, target countries that now (or could) provide a large number of tourists for the region, identify the best kinds of tours to promote, and prepare a Cascadia Travel Planner.

Joint regional trade promotion is also a precedent that should be established soon. Already, looking at Cascadia as if it were a country, the economy would be one of the genuine "economic tigers" of the Pacific Rim. Accordingly, the region should give serious consideration to organizing joint trade missions that would combine representatives of two or three Cascadian states and provinces. The Washington State Department of Trade and Economic Development's "technology missions" to Europe, which showcase both Washington state and British Columbia products there, are innovative efforts. But

Mixed Signals at the Airport

In the summer of 1991, 37 non-stop flights each week left Sea-Tac to Asia; a year later, there were only 14. Thai Airways International announced in March 1992 that it would move its Seattle headquarters to Los Angeles and cut back its daily flights to Tokyo and Bangkok; in October 1992 it eliminated those flights altogether. Thai's North American headquarters had been in Seattle since 1980, and it employed about 118 people here. In addition, United Airlines, citing low passenger loads on its daily Seattle-to-Hong Kong flights, cancelled the route and shifted the service to San Francisco (where it also received more favorable treatment). United had flown between Seattle and Hong Kong since 1983. Japan Air Lines announced in July 1992 that it would drop its twice-weekly service between Seattle and Tokyo as of November 1992. The flight had been an intermediate stop on JAL's Atlanta-Tokyo flight, but the company said Seattle was "not a viable stop" any longer. Japan Airlines reported in June 1992 that it had lost $23.3 million in the fiscal year that ended in March 1992—the first red ink since the former national flag carrier went private in 1987—and announced the elimination of 400 jobs. However, the picture is not all negative. In January 1993 two Asian airlines—Taiwan-based EVA Air, and China Eastern, based in Shanghai—announced that they would begin operating passenger and cargo flights through Sea-Tac. EVA would link Taipei, Sea-Tac and Newark. China Eastern would fly between Shanghai, Sea-Tac, Chicago and Los Angeles. In addition, it was announced that nonstop service between Sea-Tac and Moscow may begin soon, either with Aeroflot or the new private Russian airline, Transaero.

imagine the reaction in Japan or Germany if a delegation from the new U.S.-Canadian region of "Cascadia" came calling—or a "Cascadia" pavilion appeared at the 1996 World's Fair in Budapest! Wilson Parasiuk, Chairman and CEO of the British Columbia Trade Development Corporation, proposed joint B.C.-Washington State trade missions during a speech at Discovery Institute's International Seattle conference on May 6, 1993—the first time a Canadian official had made such a proposal publicly. (However, the 1993 Washington Legislature voted to merge the state Department of Trade and Economic Development with the Department of Community Development, so DTED's future ability to operate independently may be somewhat curtailed.)

In the field of education, several projects that involve Cascadia are making good progress and deserve more support. A Cascadia Alliance has been formed among the schools of architecture, urban planning and design at the Universities of Washington, Oregon and British Columbia, to work jointly on student and teacher exchanges and research, and publish a new regional journal. A committee of business school deans from the three institutions is looking at a similar arrangement. Ideally, the colleges and universities throughout the region should eliminate out-of-state tuition requirements for other students within Cascadia, so that each institution could focus on its strengths and draw students from other states and provinces.

Airports

Air transportation is key to attracting more international business, tourists, and other activities. If metropolitan Seattle is to be a successful "international gateway," and compete with other cities around the world, an improved airport is vital. Without expansion, Sea-Tac will face severe congestion and long delays by the mid-1990s, which will drive away international carriers and slow the regional economy. Any successful and competitive international community must have first-rate airport facilities and capacity, and that means expanding Sea-Tac at the very least, and eventually building or converting another field to the north or south for additional flights.

The "Flight Plan" proposal put forth last year by the 40-member Puget Sound Air Transportation Committee called for a third runway to be built at Sea-Tac by the year 2000, which would increase capacity to at least 100,000 flights a year. The plan also recommended commercial service at Everett's Paine Field by 2000, and a new airport in Pierce or Thurston County by 2010. According to some public-opinion polls, the plan had broad support among residents of the entire community. And a Port of Seattle survey in January 1993 found that King County residents supported construction of a third runway at Sea-Tac by a more than two-to-one margin, while 78 percent opposed building a new airport to replace Sea-Tac.

The committee, cosponsored by the Port of Seattle and the Puget Sound Regional Council, made its recommendations in June 1992 after more than two years of research, study, and public debate. Coincidentally, Vancouver, B.C., in June 1992

Seattle-Tacoma International Airport

announced plans to build a third runway at Vancouver International Airport to handle growing Pacific Rim traffic, which airport officials expect to grow rapidly through the 1990s. The Port of Seattle also should explore future cooperation with Vancouver, B.C. in developing more international flights to this region.

However, a coalition of serious critics continues to oppose expansion of Sea-Tac. They have formed a group called the Regional Council on Airport Affairs, which includes cities, school districts, hospital districts and community groups opposed to airport expansion. Also, a group of South King County cities, including Normandy Park, Des Moines and Burien, have earmarked public funds to hire a Washington, D.C., law firm to fight the expansion plan.

The decision is now in the hands of the Puget Sound Regional Council, which is responsible for overseeing a Regional Transportation Plan (RTP) under state and federal laws. Part of that plan is a Regional Airport System Plan (RASP), last amended in 1988. These plans are part of Vision 2020, which was adopted by the PSRC in 1991. The PSRC has conducted a thorough and objective public decision-making process, including a series of briefings, workshops, open houses, and public hearings. The PSRC in April 1993 approved a compromise authorizing a third runway at Sea-Tac by 1996, but only if a site for a major new regional airport could not be found. However, lawsuits almost inevitably will delay final action for some time.

Overall, Sea-Tac is a critical part of the regional economy, providing more than 32,000 direct or indirect jobs in 1990, with 84,000 more jobs linked to other visitor-related activities. These jobs are expected to double in number by the year 2020, and earnings to more than double from $2.1 billion to $5.6 billion.

Sea-Tac already is the nation's 22nd busiest, and the world's 33rd busiest, airport in passenger volume. The 1980s saw tremendous growth in that volume, which grew from 9.2 million passengers in 1980 to more than 16.2 million in 1990. There were nearly 18 million passengers flying in and out of Sea-Tac in 1992, which set a new record over the previous high of 16.3 million passengers in 1991 (a year when international traffic declined because of the recession and the impact of the Persian Gulf War). The Port estimates that passenger totals will rise to 24-26 million in 2000 and 37-52 million by 2020.

Total operations (takeoffs and landings combined) were 375,000 in 1992—while the airport's estimated capacity is about 400,000. At current rates of growth, that will be reached by the year 2000. The potential detrimental effects of a continuing decline in airport capacity—while such cities as Denver, Portland and Vancouver, B.C., are aggressively building new capacity—would be severe.

Cooperation with other cities in the "Cascadia" region eventually can help build international traffic, as well. One promising marketing concept now under discussion: Persuade international carriers to alternate daily first-destination stops in Seattle and Vancouver, B.C., with a second (also alternating) stop at the other city. This would give carriers a much larger effective target population for marketing efforts.

Finding ways to retain international air routes at Sea-Tac must be a high priority for the metropolitan region's leaders during the 1990s and beyond. And expanding the capacity of Sea-Tac to prevent congestion and avoid delays must be a first step toward that goal. Granted, the worldwide recession has caused a slowdown in number of flights, but the volume is almost certain to increase in years ahead and this region must be prepared to compete or it will be left behind.

Ports/Trade

4. RECOMMENDATION: The Ports of Puget Sound should continue strengthening their strategic alliance to promote greater efficiency in marketing the region internationally and making optimum use of each port's assets.

In the increasingly competitive global marketplace, it is vital to have more cooperation among Puget Sound area ports. Increased cooperation, indeed, reflects what is happening in the transportation industry worldwide. The Puget Sound ports' market share of West Coast cargo has fallen recently, even though each port has set volume records. A lack of coordination can lead to overbuilding of capital inventories, as well.

There have been encouraging signs of cooperation in recent months. Both the Ports of Seattle and Tacoma are helping to finance the new state/ports office in Paris. During a recent trade mission, the Port of Everett used the Port of Seattle's office in Tokyo. Also, in June 1993 the "Puget Sound Ports Group," a previously informal alliance among the ports of Anacortes, Bellingham, Everett, Olympia, Port Angeles, Seattle and Tacoma, formalized a cooperative agreement. Primarily a marketing organization, the group has published an attractive booklet on "The Gateway Ports of Puget Sound." While the ports will avoid rate-setting and remain competitive, they will try to increase business for all. For example, in late September the group will sponsor a joint mission to the Soviet Far East.

The vision of a combined Seattle-Tacoma Port Authority, which was endorsed in the draft version of this report, lacks support and is unlikely to be realized anytime soon. Tacoma, which has been highly competitive with Seattle in the past and will continue to be so because of its large land holdings near the waterfront, has been reluctant to formalize any relationship. The only way to build regional trust, therefore, is through step-by-step efforts such as the Ports Group.

Pooled resources can lead to greater recognition of the region and efficiencies in international marketing and use of public funds, to a greater return for taxpayers on their investment in port facilities, and to increased political and marketing clout.

In the meantime, regardless of rate competition, all Puget Sound area ports should play more active roles in promoting international trade for the metropolitan region. The port commissions and the executive directors should, to the greatest extent possible, become strong spokespersons for the concept of increasing economic development through more international trade.

Tourism

5. RECOMMENDATION: International tourism should be given a higher priority within existing tourism promotional efforts at the federal, state and local levels. Meanwhile, a consortium of business and government tourism experts should prepare a factual justification for state and local governments to increase this region's relatively small current investment in tourism promotion.

As it is, international tourism (and tourism generally) represents an underutilized source for tax-revenue growth and the creation of badly needed

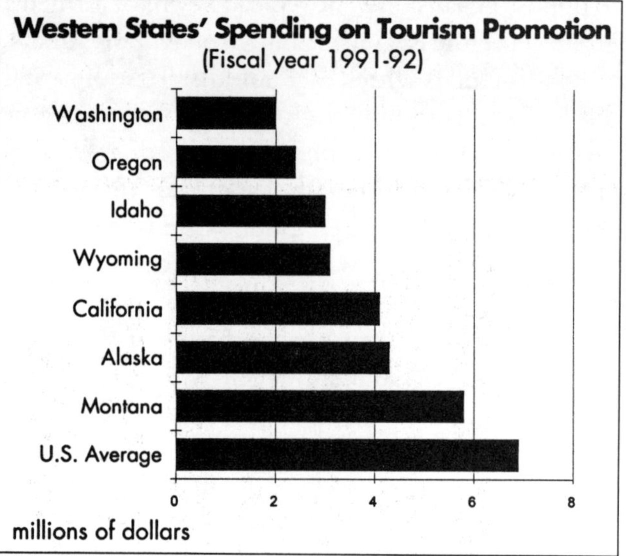

low- and medium-skill-level jobs. Failure in this realm puts us at a competitive disadvantage with other areas of the world.

In the mid-1970s, futurist Herman Kahn predicted that travel and tourism would be the world's largest industry by the year 2000. He was off by nearly a decade: It actually became the world's largest industry in 1991. It is the United States' third-largest industry, with $344 million in gross receipts, more than general merchandise retailing. It is the country's largest "export" — 43 million visitors from other countries spent $64 billion in the U.S. in 1992. Nationally, international tourism is growing by about 15 percent annually, while domestic tourism is growing by only about 6 percent a year. As the rest of the world grows more prosperous, foreign tourists will want to visit the United States in ever-increasing numbers, and this state should attract a larger share of them.

However, Washington State's tourism promotion efforts have been seriously deficient in recent years. Washington was 49th out of 50 states in per capita spending on tourism promotion (less than 50 cents per resident, compared to $18 in Alaska, for instance). Nonetheless, the Washington Legislature had cut the budget for tourism promotion by 35 percent over the five year period from 1988-92. This was despite the fact that tourism is already the state's fourth largest industry—generating $5.5 billion in economic activity in 1992 and providing jobs for almost 100,000 Washingtonians in nearly 14,000 businesses—and has the potential to become much larger in the future. Oregon, Idaho and Montana do far more to attract tourists, as does British Columbia. The latter's tourism-promotion

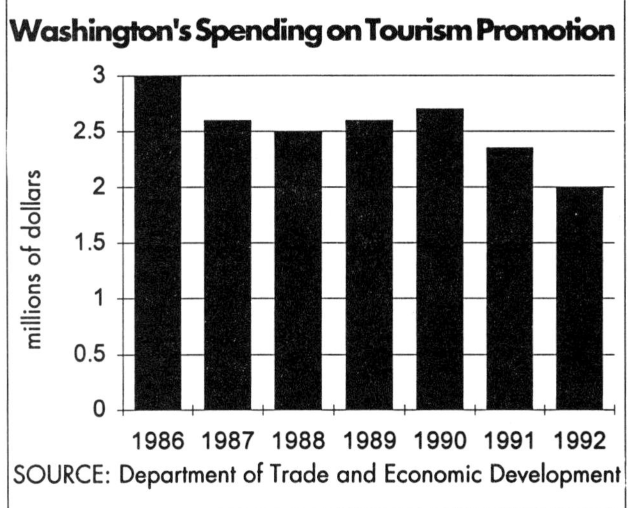

budget is 10 times that of Washington State's despite our larger population base.

The 1993 Legislature, to its credit, raised the biennial (1993-95) tourism-promotion budget to $5.5 million. But Washington's 12-person Tourism Divison is still one of the nation's smallest and is struggling to keep up with the demand for information. Washington has been ranked among the nation's top 10 tourist destination states in at least three polls in the past year, and it ranks 20th in tourism revenues.

In 1990, international visitors accounted for about 2.9 million, or more than 8 percent, of the 34.4 million visits to Washington state. Most of these—2.4 million—were from Canada. The other approximately 530,000 were from overseas. International tourists have been about 8 percent of the state's tourists for the past four years, but their numbers have climbed steadily. In 1986, they were only 6 percent, and in 1987, 7 percent.

There is good evidence that tourism promotion pays off. In 1990, of the $5.3 billion that visitors spent here, adding $222 million to the state in sales and other tax revenues, a healthy percentage was spent by international tourists. According to estimates by the U.S. Travel and Tourism Administration (USTTA), the international tourists who visited Washington state in 1990 spent about $837 million. Foreign visitors spend more than other tourists—an average of $1,480 per visitor per trip, according to USTTA estimates. Japanese tourists spend an average of $4,600 per trip.

Washington ranks as the third most popular state in the U.S. for Canadian tourists, the seventh most popular state for total international tourists, and the 14th most popular for overseas tourists. In 1990 the Seattle-King County region received $2.3 billion, or nearly 43 percent, of the $5.3 billion tourism dollars spent in the state. Full-time employment generated by tourism is estimated at 42,000 in King County, with more than 10,000 jobs in the hotel and motel industry alone. Imagine how much higher those numbers could be with an aggressive tourism-promotion program!

Although international tourists now account for less than 10 percent of all tourists, foreign markets are expected to grow the fastest. The International Tourism Committee (made up of the Seattle King County Convention and Visitors Bureau, the Port of Seattle, the state Trade Department's Tourism Development Division, and representatives of major hotels) has targeted Japan, the United Kingdom, eastern Canada, Taiwan and South Korea as places where the state can increase its current international tourist market share in the next 5 to 10 years.

If international tourism is to fulfill its potential in becoming a larger part of total regional tourism, the area also should, among other things:

❏ Encourage all reasonable efforts to make downtown areas safer and less threatening to international tourists through crime-prevention programs and attempts to diminish aggressive panhandling, public drunkenness and substance abuse that scare tourists away.

❏ Be more sensitive and accommodating to international tourists through improvements at Sea-Tac Airport, train stations, bus depots, ferry terminals and other main entry points, as well as in area mass-transit systems and major shopping areas. Better assistance at the airport and more multilingual signage and translated brochures should be available to help international visitors. And luggage carts should be provided free to international-arrival passengers, who often do not have U.S. currency in correct denominations to pay for them.

❑ Publish a new "Living in Seattle" guidebook on the Seattle metropolitan area for foreign businesspeople and temporary residents that would be available in several languages and provide basic information on how to get around, where to shop, eat, tour, etc. Use the Japan America Society's handbook, and those of other cities, as models. Such a guidebook, among other things, would help involve foreign residents in the educational and cultural activities of the region.

❑ Support the Downtown Seattle Association/Seattle-King County Convention & Visitors Bureau's promotion of Greater Seattle in Vancouver, B.C., Western Canada and other Pacific Northwest states to attract tourists and visitors, and use that as a model to do similar programs elsewhere.

❑ Encourage local banks to offer more convenient foreign-currency exchange windows downtown for international visitors. Also, discourage "No Canadian Money" signs, which are offensive and detrimental to business.

❑ Consider moving the Visitor Information Center from its current location in the Washington State Convention & Trade Center to a more visible and strategic spot. Alternatively, a branch office of the Visitor Center should be opened at Westlake, Pike Place Market, or on the Waterfront, and fully equipped with multilingual literature, maps, videos, information assistants, a hotel reservation service, etc. Even a seasonal branch open in the summer months would be helpful.

❑ Encourage more joint U.S.-Canadian tourism-promotion programs for "Cascadia," involving British Columbia, Washington, Oregon, Idaho and other states and provinces. The "two-nation vacation" idea is especially attractive to European and Asian tourists.

❑ When international delegations or trade missions are in town, encourage government offices, hotels and downtown office buildings to fly the flags of the visiting nations, which can be a simple but effective means of making the guests feel welcome.

Quality of Life

6. RECOMMENDATION: In any urban area, a high quality of life entails a harmony—not a constant war—between economic and environmental health. Thus, Seattle metropolitan area governments, and the state, should streamline their land-use and physical-development processes.

The metropolitan Seattle area is widely known for its good quality of life, which means a combination of economic opportunities and environmental amenities. To be a great international community, we must maintain that balance. Other cities have lost it. Not only have their reputations worldwide suffered as a result, but their citizens have suffered from a diminished quality of life.

Borrowing from the examples of other notably livable and economically prosperous areas of the world, area governments should streamline the physical-development process to assure greater legal predictability, timeliness, human scale, utility and natural beauty. Good design, reliable permit standards, amenities (parks, landscaping, open space), and public agencies that work cooperatively together are jointly conducive to a strategy of international competitiveness.

Studies over many years show that while people in our metropolitan area may differ over issues of land preservation and growth management, there is relative agreement over the qualities that make for an agreeable urban existence: dense enough downtown living to support a strong transit system, retail core and cultural vitality; public safety; definable neighborhoods; efficient local government; and provident planning, with good design and ample green space for recreation and beauty.

Too often, carefully considered plans that take all such elements into account are derailed because the environmental and/or building permit process is manipulated in a perverse manner to defeat rather than to facilitate democratic oversight. Also, over-regulation and duplication among government agencies sometimes make it ruinously expensive for businesses to establish themselves here or expand. Government's role should be to encourage sound development and job creation through a clear, rational planning process.

The survey that accompanied the *Fortune* magazine study cited earlier made it clear that our area would have been still better favored but for its perceived anti-business climate. The answer is for

If a balance is struck between high-quality development and open-space preservation, the whole region will benefit.

government, business, labor and advocacy groups to work out common project guidelines early on, then defend them in the common interest.

Sometimes, for example, this region tends to emphasize preserving wilderness, forests and rural areas while neglecting improvements in urban areas where people actually live. This is not to say that new urban areas cannot be developed, but they should be planned on a human scale with human values—including natural beauty, shopping and services. Seattle Mayor Norm Rice's proposal to develop "urban villages" is an approach that deserves refinement and support.

Such techniques as screening parking lots with shrubs and trees, undergrounding electrical-utility wiring, and planting trees along freeways and other arterials, can accomplish a great deal to make cities seem more livable and, in the best sense, civilized. Civic leader Jim Ellis' proposal to screen the I-90 corridor with trees, parks and open space in a "Mountains to Sound Greenway" is a particularly praiseworthy concept.

Consider many of the great cities in Europe,

some of which were virtually in ruins after World War II, but now seem more livable than most American cities. They achieved that quality by carefully planning their downtown areas for people, with a mix of buildings and open space. Like such cities in Germany and elsewhere, metropolitan Seattle should recognize that when it improves the urban environment, it also helps the regional economy. The goal is not to stop development, but to shape it. Put simply, quality pays off. If a balance is struck between high-quality development in urban areas, and preservation of open space in developed outlying areas, the whole region will benefit.

It is possible to be an "international city" with a degraded environment, of course: consider Bangkok, Taipei and Mexico City. But ideally, internationalism should create a demand—and generate the resources—for prudent environmental improvements. Metropolitan Seattle should strive to be like one of the attractive places—Vancouver, B.C., Sydney, Florence and Heidelberg (with its parking garages underneath ancient squares) come to mind. Such cities have solved some of the environmental problems that otherwise would have reduced their appeal and impeded their economies. It is indeed possible to have both a clean environment and a healthy economy, and metropolitan Seattle should set a goal of becoming the world's prime example of that ideal.

Education

(NOTE: See also Recommendations 17-22.)

7. RECOMMENDATION: By the year 2000, the metropolitan region's school districts should increase by 50 percent the number of students who take foreign languages, and the average number of years they study each language. Increased use of software language instruction can greatly speed this process, hold down costs, and improve proficiency.

Some have suggested setting a goal of having *every* high-school student in the Seattle metropolitan area speak a foreign language by graduation, but that seems overly ambitious and even unnecessary. Still, improving foreign-language training in public schools must become a much higher priority from now on if our area is to compete successfully with communities in Europe and Asia.

Although Washington State is Number 1 in the U.S. in per capita trade, it is Number 25 in the percentage of high-school students who study foreign languages, according to a 1990 survey by the American Council on Teaching of Foreign Languages. The region's citizens should recognize the crucial importance of improving K-12 language classes as a way to boost international trade and tourism—and thus help the regional economy. They also should recognize that, absent improvement in foreign-language proficiency locally, jobs here that benefit from such proficiency will tend to be filled by people imported from other regions and countries—a lost opportunity for our own youth.

Currently, only about 40 percent of high-school students in Washington state study a foreign language, and then for an average of only 2 years— not long enough to gain fluency. The goal should be to increase the percentage to at least 60 percent, and to raise the average number of years studied to at least 3 years. Moreover, at least 20 percent of all students should graduate with genuine fluency in a foreign language, not just a rudimentary knowledge. In order to accomplish this, it will be necessary to start language education in the elementary schools, because achieving fluency takes years of study and practice. It should be possible for students to take up to 12 years of major languages such as German, Japanese, Spanish, French, Russian and Mandarin Chinese. It would be better for schools to teach these major languages well than to offer a smorgasbord of many languages–each offering little more than an introduction. (For example, Highland Park Elementary School in West Seattle has a model program to teach Russian to young students. The program was about to be cancelled due to budget cutbacks, but was saved partly because of concerns raised by parents who cited this report and Discovery Institute's May 6 conference to school administrators.)

The state is making an effort to encourage more foreign-language classes in public schools statewide, and with some success in recent years. The latest annual survey of course offerings and enrollments in schools statewide found that eight major languages

are taught in Washington high schools: Spanish, French, German, Japanese, Russian, Latin, Chinese and Swedish. A total of 92,843 high-school students were enrolled in language classes during the 1991-92 school year, which amounted to 39.9 percent of all students in grades 9 through 12 statewide. Those numbers are up from 80,878 (36.1 percent) of students in 1990-91, and 78,337 (34.2 percent) in 1989-90.

Still, compared to other states in the U.S., Washington is about average. According to the national survey by the American Council on the Teaching of Foreign Languages (ACTFL), 38.4 percent of all U.S. high-school students in grades 9-12 were studying a foreign language in the fall of 1990. In the ACTFL survey, Washington's level of foreign-language instruction (then 36.1 percent) was lower than that of two of the other top five trading states: California (40 percent) and New York (63.5 percent), although it was higher than that of Texas (33.8 percent) and Michigan (28.9 percent). Although Washington's percentage for 1991-92 was up closer to 40 percent, it still should be higher.

And compared to other countries, of course, U.S. language-study rates are disturbingly low. In most European countries, taking at least one foreign language is mandatory, not elective, starting in the 7th grade or earlier. In Japan, English is required from elementary school through high school. Thus close to 100 percent of these students study a language, usually English and often another as well.

A new opportunity for increasing language instruction without adding greatly to school budgets is afforded by emerging computer software technology for individualized learning. Overall, sales of educational software are booming—up 50 percent in 1992 over the previous year. This technology, which is developing rapidly and will soon incorporate "virtual reality," also will aid older people who suddenly find the need to pick up language instruction for a job assignment. The technology should be adopted as quickly as possible by higher-education institutions as well as the common schools. The state education reform program still being refined by the Legislature should certainly include expanding this technology, with a goal of speeding its adoption in all of the schools. Seattle metropolitan area schools must not miss this opportunity.

8. RECOMMENDATION: The administration of the University of Washington should give a higher priority to the U.W.'s extensive international activities, encourage the Vice Provost to better coordinate these activities, and seek more resources to support them.

In their book, *Missing the Boat: The Failure to Internationalize American Higher Education,* (Cambridge University Press, 1991), Craufurd D. Goodwin and Michael Nacht wrote: "The internationalization of U.S. colleges and universities that is required for the 1990s is far more profound than that accomplished in earlier decades....The internationalization of the Nineties cannot be the responsibility of a few on campus who are assigned to do those foreign tasks. It must become part of the central mission of an institution, not just a piece of presidential rhetoric or some phrases in the case for reaccreditation."

Goodwin and Nacht concluded that just as the U.S. private sector has been compelled to become more globally oriented in recent years, American higher education must do the same. This must happen quickly if the adjustment is to be made from a position of strength rather than weakness, as was the case for much of the U.S. manufacturing industry, they argued. With support from the Council for International Exchange of Scholars and the Pew Charitable Trusts, they studied the international activities of 37 American colleges and universities— including the University of Washington. The study's goal was to find ways to increase the number of faculty and student exchanges, and to incorporate international dimensions into curriculums.

In their review of the University of Washington's international activities, Craufurd and Nacht correctly noted that the U.W. was especially strong in Soviet and East Asian studies, foreign languages and the natural sciences and that the U.W. Law School has special expertise in comparative legal studies, including Japanese contract law.

Even so, many observers believe that the University of Washington's international connections have come about almost in spite of, not because of, the administrative policies of the U.W. International activities are scattered throughout various schools and departments, and lack central coordination or consistent encouragement from the administration.

Kane Hall, University of Washington

A June 1991 report, "International Activities at the University of Washington," by the U.W.'s Foreign Study Office, concluded that historically, most international activity at the U.W. has been initiated by faculty interest rather than by administration directive. This is true of exchange programs, joint research projects, and international conferences and colloquia.

The problems of the U.W.'s relatively neglected international activities should receive the direct attention of the U.W. president and the Board of Regents. In 1993 a new person, Carol M. Eastman, was named to the position of Dean of the Graduate School, with the concurrent title of Vice Provost and responsibility for acting as "international coordinator," which is a promising development. Eastman is taking an aggressive role in better coordinating international activity on campus. In addition, an International Resource Group has been meeting regularly and is building a computerized database of international activity including a list of visiting scholars and exchange programs; its eventual goal is to link up with community organizations as well.

Such efforts also could provide a boost for the U.W.'s international Outreach Programs, some of which are currently quite good but are grossly underfunded and do not have the impact in the community that they might. These programs should receive increased support and be expanded to play a greater role in the metropolitan region. For example, the U.W. needs to work more closely with the Seattle Public Schools, and other regional K-12 programs, not only to improve the quality of education of incoming students but also to help raise educational standards and performance in general.

There is fine talent at the university, but the institution could provide more to the community in terms of international expertise. Such universities as Harvard, Stanford and the University of California at Berkeley are examples of institutions with closer ties to their communities and active working relationships with local governments, business and private nonprofit organizations concerned with international trade and international affairs. In general, the U.W. is not yet fulfilling its potential as a resource for the increasingly international community in which it is located. A greater public effort to help the U.W. see its larger role in the community—along with pressure on the Legislature to provide the university with the resources it needs— is overdue.

> 9. RECOMMENDATION: The University of Washington should make the Henry M. Jackson School of International Studies a true regional flagship of internationalism by increasing its resources and making it an independent school with its own dean.

The Henry M. Jackson School of International Studies, which began as a small department in 1910 and was renamed after the late senator in 1983, is a focus of internationalism on the campus. With a full-time faculty of 24 members, it offers 11 undergraduate programs and nine graduate programs. It also sponsors conferences, speakers, career

Drumheller Fountain, University of Washington

workshops and other public service activities. The number of faculty is 36, including those with joint appointments in other departments who teach half-time at the Jackson School. Faculty totals about 100 if one includes members of other departments or colleges who participate in various Jackson School programs, seminars and colloquia, or who teach courses that count for credit toward degrees the School offers.

The School has six federally funded National Resource Centers to provide training and continuing education for teachers, business people and the public. In comparison, Columbia University has seven such centers and the University of California has six; the Universities of Wisconsin and Indiana, five each; Cornell, Stanford and Michigan, four each.

The Jackson School has an excellent record of preparing students for the U.S. Foreign Service, and is highly regarded by the State Department. The School's Outreach Program includes a wide range of public lectures, teachers' workshops, evening classes, summer institutes, speakers' bureaus, museum exhibits, concerts and film series. It also offers "Second Saturdays," a series of day-long seminars on regional and international topics, and "Mosaics," training sessions directed at teachers of kindergarten through 9th grade. The School often brings leading national and international statesmen and scholars to the campus for public lectures and seminars with students.

But the Jackson School, though an invaluable regional resource, in recent years, through a combination of inadequate funding and inconsistent leadership, was allowed to slip a notch or two in quality and reputation. The appointment in August 1991 of a new director, Nicholas Lardy, was a good start toward reversing that trend. But much remains to be done.

Preferably, the Jackson School—which is now part of the College of Arts and Sciences—should be a separate and independent school, like the Graduate School of Public Affairs (which also is doing an increasingly commendable job of training its students for international careers and also deserves more support). That would help give the Jackson School the prestige and authority that it deserves. The School also should someday have its own building, with facilities to receive international visitors and meeting rooms to host international gatherings. Ideally, such a site might be "endowed" by a local foundation, which would give its name to the center. This building also could house the International Students Center and Outreach Programs.

Compared to other schools and colleges at the U.W., the Jackson School is underfunded. With 481 students (graduate and undergraduate) and a core faculty of 36, it had a total budget of $3.8 million in 1990-91 ($1.7 million from the state and $2.1 million from external sources). In comparison, in the same academic year the College of Forest Resources, with 369 students and 60 faculty members, had a budget of $14.9 million ($4.8 million from the state, the rest from external sources). The College of Oceanography and Fisheries, with 440 students and 150 faculty, had a $47 million

budget ($8.7 million from the state).

The state currently is not providing adequate support to the U.W. in general, and the Jackson School in particular. This must change in order for the Jackson School to take its rightful place as one of the top international studies schools in the country, if not the world. As many observers have noted, a school's effectiveness all comes down to having adequate resources. Without them, it can't do much. When thinking about the proper level of funding for studies on international affairs and global trade, administrators and legislators should bear in mind this question: Where are the job needs of our future? Much of this report, of course, argues that our future success resides in better training our workforce for international competitiveness.

High-Speed Rail

10. RECOMMENDATION: Metropolitan regional officials should support study efforts now under way to build a high-speed rail line from Portland to Seattle to Vancouver, B.C., with connecting links to the airports in each city.

Given that more than 20 percent of the operations at Sea-Tac Airport are commuter flights to Portland and Vancouver, B.C., a high-speed rail line linked to the airport(s) would provide an alternative for passengers, especially if it were competitive in time and price of travel. Members of the 1992 European Study Mission were especially impressed by a system in Germany, where Lufthansa Airlines runs its own train linking the Frankfurt Airport to other cities including Bonn and Stuttgart. It is even possible to check baggage through to a final destination on the air-rail system, which is considered a model worldwide.

The U.S. Department of Transportation in October 1992 approved the designation of a new high-speed passenger-rail corridor from the U.S.-Canadian border to Eugene, Ore. This increases the prospect of more federal funding for high-speed rail service along the I-5 corridor linking the Pacific Northwest's major cities. Initially, a total of $500,000 in federal funds are being allocated to Washington and Oregon under the Intermodal Surface

Transportation Efficiency Act. This is only a beginning: the state High Speed Ground Transportation Steering Committee has estimated that building a 334-mile north-south system connecting Portland and Vancouver, B.C., could cost $9 billion to $12 billion if it were a French- or Japanese-style "bullet train" capable of speeds from 150-200 miles per hour. An enhanced conventional train that would run at 80-150 mph on existing tracks would be less expensive and perhaps more feasible. Again, the private sector should be given an opportunity to take part, if not take over, this scheme.

At the least, there should be basic improvements to Amtrak service within the corridor, and continuing support for the concept of "intermodalism," which can help break down the barriers between travel by car, bus, train, ferry, and plane. The Transportation Department funds include $150,000 to Seattle to study the concept of rebuilding King Street station as a regional intermodal transfer terminal, which is an excellent idea worth aggressively pursuing.

In the fall of 1994, regular rail service between Seattle and Vancouver, B.C., will resume for the first time since 1981. The U.S. and Canada reached an agreement in July 1993 to eliminate a lengthy stop at the border for customs and immigration inspections. Seattle Mayor Norm Rice and U.S. Rep. Al Swift, among others, had been pushing for the restoration of Amtrak service. A joint U.S.-Canadian task force has been formed to work toward improving the Amtrak rail system so it can accommodate faster trains. The Washington State Transportation Commission recently was impressed by a demonstration of the Swedish-built X2000 train, designed to run on electricity at 135-150 mph. But about $1.2 billion would be required to upgrade crossings and electrify tracks between Vancouver, B.C., and Portland.

The Cascadia Corridor Transportation Task Force, a Discovery Institute effort, is working toward improving rail service as well, and has helped organize meetings of the mayors of Seattle, Tacoma, Portland and Vancouver, B.C. The U.S.-Canada Free Trade Agreement has made this stretch of land an important corridor of commerce with enormous potential for future economic development. A high-speed rail line could tie the region together, provide great economic benefits, and be an invaluable international marketing tool and attraction for tourists and businesspeople.

20 More Steps Toward a Globally Competitive Community

Transportation

11. RECOMMENDATION: A better regional transportation system is a vital element of metropolitan Seattle's long-term global competitiveness, because people, goods and services will tend to move elsewhere if congestion becomes too severe. Therefore, the metropolitan area should at last decide on a regional transportation plan that will meet long-term growth needs and alleviate commuter and commercial gridlock.

This report cannot and will not outline a precise description of what elements should be included in that plan. There is an urgent need for much more debate on potential features and costs, and eventually a public vote must be held. Encouragingly, however, the community appears to be gradually moving toward a decision on such a plan.

In October 1992, after three years of study, the Joint Regional Policy Committee, made up of representatives from King, Pierce, and Snohomish counties, released a draft system plan for a proposed Regional Transit Project (RTP) costing at least $9 billion. This would be one of the most expensive capital works projects ever undertaken in this state. An 88-mile rail rapid transit system is anticipated from Everett through Seattle to Tacoma, with a branch to the Eastside along the I-90 corridor. The plan would add 380 lane miles of HOV (high occupancy vehicle) lanes for buses and carpools, and include related ramp improvements. More than 2,300 buses and 13 maintenance and operation facilities would be added, along with a 40-mile-long commuter railroad line that would run on existing tracks between Tacoma and Seattle. Exact transit corridor alignments and project phasing have yet to be worked out.

The plan calls for a Regional Transit Authority (RTA) to be created by the state Legislature in 1993, with the approval of the three county councils. Indeed, all three councils now have approved the RTA (the King County Council by a 5-4 vote in July 1993). The RTA will be a three-county taxing district that will collect and disperse public funds and oversee the system. Funding for the project remains to be determined, but a combination of federal, state and local taxes, and some private funds, is envisioned. Local taxes would probably have to be raised, through a combination of a local sales tax on gas, an increase in the motor vehicle excise tax, and perhaps a local option gas tax. Together, these sources would provide about $320 million a year from the three-county area, with the impact on a typical King County household of roughly $140 a year for 30 years, according to the Seattle-King County Municipal League.

However, there is considerable doubt that voters will approve such an elaborate and expensive mass-transit system if it is presented to them on the ballot anytime soon. The Greater Seattle Chamber of Commerce in March 1993 declined to endorse the proposal, expressing valid concern that the huge cost would preclude other badly needed road, bus and rail improvements. Any vote probably should be postponed until fall 1994, because an early ballot defeat would set back the cause for many years.

In addition, at least one reasonable alternative proposal has already surfaced. A citizens' group called SMART, for Sound Metropolitan Area Rapid Transit, in January 1993 proposed a less ambitious plan that would place more emphasis on improving bus service and carpool lanes, with a rail line from Seattle to Bellevue, or from downtown Seattle to Sea-Tac Airport or the University District. The group also suggests more subsidies to increase bus ridership and a parking price structure that discourages automobile use. They called the RTP "fundamentally flawed" because it is "too big and too rigid."

King County Executive Tim Hill, in his annual "state of the county" address, also called the regional transit plan overly ambitious and suggested doing it in phases to lessen the impact on taxpayers. He recommended that the first leg of any light-rail system link Seattle to the Eastside. However, Seattle Mayor Norm Rice, in his annual "state of the city" address, endorsed the regional plan and added a new suggestion: a network of small shuttle buses that would better link neighborhoods to transit stops. He called it LINC (Local Initiative for Neighborhood Circulation), and estimated it would add up to $160 million a year in operating costs. Whatever form it takes, a regional transit plan should be phased in gradually, use the least expensive increments first and not consider light rail as a panacea, because it's not.

Critics cannot be faulted for challenging the assumptions of the Regional Transit Plan and encouraging public debate on the issue. That's the best way for the region to spark creativity and arrive at a final plan. But even if voters turn down a bond issue, such a defeat during a period of general tax hikes at state and federal levels should not discourage officials from later attempts. Solutions are necessary and will not become cheaper with the passage of time.

Another development that could affect the RTP was the Burlington Northern Railroad's announcement in January 1993 that it will begin running a commuter train along existing tracks between Seattle and Everett. It said the line could carry 30,000 to 50,000 people a day for about 5 percent of the cost of a more elaborate new light-rail system, and be operating in about two years compared to the 15 years it could take to get a new system finished. The BN scheme would run 32 trains a day from the King Street Station in downtown Seattle along Puget Sound to Everett, and include stops near the Pike Place Market, Edmonds, Mukilteo, and other places. Passengers could connect to ferries and bus lines, including

Snohomish County's Community Transit, which now carries about 6,000 people a day. Obviously, such a private-sector initiative, if feasible, is highly desirable on grounds of cost and accountability, and should be encouraged.

Cruise Ships

12. RECOMMENDATION: Washington State's congressional delegation should strongly support new federal legislation to allow foreign-flag cruise ships to travel between U.S. ports.

One tourist sector that has long been underdeveloped in metropolitan Seattle is the cruise-ship industry. Because of the federal Passenger Service Act of 1886, which prohibits foreign-flag passenger ships from one-way service between U.S. ports, most cruise ships (which are nearly all foreign-flagged) do not stop in Seattle or other Washington state ports. Efforts to amend the law have been blocked in Congress by labor unions and domestic cargo-ship interests who fear any changes might detrimentally affect the U.S. merchant fleet. They fear that any amendments to the Passenger Service Act might undermine the Jones Act, which similarly requires that all cargo traffic between U.S. ports can move only on U.S.-flagged ships with American crews.

Thus, because of a century-plus-old law, Seattle is prevented from being a port of embarkation for cruise ships traveling to Alaska. As a result, this area loses millions of dollars and thousands of jobs to Vancouver, B.C., which has become a center of the lucrative Alaska cruise-ship industry. More than 300,000 passengers now travel to Alaska by ship each summer, most of them departing from Vancouver, B.C.—although the majority initially land at Sea-Tac Airport before traveling by bus or car to Canada.

Encouraging efforts are underway to change the laws to allow foreign passenger ships to travel between U.S. ports, which would make it possible for cruise ships to Alaska to depart from Seattle. Rep. Jolene Unsoeld, D-Wash., plans to introduce legislation to allow such trips if a foreign ship's owners commit to begin building a vessel in the United States to replace it within three years. The bill also contains tax incentives and other provisions to increase cruise activity from U.S. ports while increasing U.S. jobs and stimulating American shipbuilding.

One Canadian government study estimated that the cruise trade from the port of Vancouver generates about $350 million and over 3,000 additional jobs. More than 200 times each summer season, a cruise ship leaves Vancouver on its way to Alaska. The Vancouver-Alaska cruise-ship industry is growing

The Seattle area's potential to increase its business in international conventions and trade shows is considerable.

by 6 to 10 percent annually. And 90 percent of the passengers are American.

Many members of Congress have been hesitant to endorse any changes in the Passenger Service Act, apparently reluctant to risk the wrath of powerful maritime unions, who fear job losses for their members. However, the change actually would create union jobs as U.S. ports opened up to passenger trade. Travel industry leaders also have indicated they would applaud the policy change, which, in addition to Seattle, could benefit the cities of Portland, San Francisco, Los Angeles, San Diego, Galveston, Boston and New York.

Of course, changes in the laws won't guarantee that cruise-ships lines will move all their business to Seattle. For one thing, it takes a half-day longer to get to Alaska from here than from Vancouver, B.C., and that's a significant difference for a five-day or even seven-day cruise. Also, Vancouver has tried hard to please the industry there, building a new Canada Place Terminal in 1986 and taking other steps to improve capacity and accessibility for cruise-ship passengers. Still, every effort should be made in the metropolitan Seattle region to attract more of this business.

Another promising development is the concept

of "repositioning" of ships that would stop here on their way to Alaska and Vancouver, B.C., for the summer season. The Port of Seattle expects nine repositioning cruise ship stops in 1993, up from seven the previous year. Also, the Port is building a new cruise-ship terminal as part of its waterfront redevelopment project, which should make a big difference in attracting cruise lines to stop here in the future. Some Vancouver officials, indeed, believe that if Seattle is able to attract more cruise ships, the overall growth in traffic will ultimately help both cities.

Conferences

13. RECOMMEN-DATION: The Seattle metropolitan area should establish itself in the 1990s as one of the world's leading meeting centers. The Port of Seattle's new International Conference Center at Pier 66 should be built to the highest feasible standards and its opening should be used as the centerpiece of a new joint public-private promotional campaign to attract more international diplomatic, trade, professional, medical, environmental, high-tech and other groups.

The metropolitan area has an enviable array of convention facilities, including the Washington State Convention and Trade Center, the Tacoma Convention Center—and soon, Bellevue's new Meydenbauer Center and the Port's International Conference Center—not to mention private facilities available at many local hotels. The region should capitalize on this advantageous position by better coordinating and marketing its facilities. It should stress the image of metropolitan Seattle as an attractive and comfortable place to meet, with first-class sites and state-of-the-art equipment.

As part of its current $57 million Central Waterfront Redevelopment Project, the Port of Seattle has built new headquarters at Pier 69 to replace the aging and inadequate building at Pier 66. The latter will be replaced by an International

Washington State Convention and Trade Center

Conference Center with state-of-the-art simultaneous translation facilities—one of only two such facilities on the North American continent (although Vancouver, B.C., is about to build one, too). The Port Commission scaled down the size of the conference center from a capacity of 700 people to about 250, with secondary rooms for another 150, because a consulting group warned that a larger center might not be used to capacity.

This site will draw small- to mid-sized gatherings from all over the world in such fields as medicine, diplomacy, high technology and communications, as well as many domestic meetings. To have such a facility will be a significant addition to metropolitan Seattle's status as an international community. We would like the Port to consider how a permanent translating staff might be developed from conference center usage, since the existence of a team of translators skilled at international (United Nations) level of ability will help attract still more business and create still more jobs in this field. The waterfront project also includes a cruise-ship terminal, maritime museum, small-boat harbor, restaurant, bookstore-cafe, and space for two fish-processing companies.

Construction is nearly complete on the new Meydenbauer Center in Bellevue, which is expected to draw considerable business to the Eastside when it opens in September 1993. By mid-1993, about three dozen conventions had already been booked at the center, with a total estimated attendance of more than 35,000 people. Although it will focus primarily on local and regional gatherings, the center is drawing some international groups. Tacoma's International Convention Center, which is administered by the Sheraton Tacoma Hotel, draws at least one or two international groups annually, although its market is primarily domestic.

The potential for the Seattle area to increase its business in large international conventions and trade shows is considerable. The Washington State Convention and Trade Center (WSCTC), which has concentrated primarily on local, regional and national markets since it opened in 1988, wants to attract more international gatherings in the future. The center is tapping the international market in two ways:

❏ First, in 1990 it joined two major worldwide organizations of convention facilities. One, the Association Internationale des Palais de Congres, is primarily European; the WSCTC is one of only six U.S. members. The other group, the Asia-Pacific Exhibition and Convention Council, focuses on the Pacific Rim—and the WSCTC is the only U.S. member of that group.

❏ Second, the convention center markets itself by using local educational institutions such as the University of Washington and other colleges and universities to spread the word, especially targeting medical, high technology and scientific gatherings.

Center officials believe that attendance from international delegates has increased, but there are no hard statistics to prove that because few convention groups compile (or are willing to share) detailed demographic information on their delegates. Estimates of increased international attendance are based largely on observations by center staff and requests for interpreters and guides. Madison, Wisconsin, with a population less than half that of Seattle's, designed a campaign to attract more international meetings, and now has about 200 each year, although many of them are relatively small. Granted, the global convention market of large international organizations may be relatively limited, but it is surely possible to attract more groups that have international participants.

The announcement that the ministerial conference of the Asian Pacific Economic Cooperation (APEC) forum will be held in Seattle in November 1993, and President Clinton's subsequent invitation to the heads of state to join him here for a leadership conference, is an encouraging example of what's possible. The group's members include the United States, Japan, China, South Korea, Taiwan, Canada, Australia, New Zealand, Thailand, Hong Kong, Indonesia, Malaysia, Singapore, Brunei and the Philippines. Together,

the members account for 46 percent of world economic production and one-third of world trade. Bob Kapp, president of the Washington Council on International Trade, played a key role in bringing the APEC meeting to Seattle. It is expected to draw hundreds of top officials, trade experts and international press.

One reason the international convention market here should grow: International travel, as described above, is growing steadily each year, while domestic travel is relatively flat. The more people that come here from other countries, and see what the metropolitan area has to offer, the more who will want to come back for professional gatherings. Also, the more convention centers in the region (up to a point, of course), the better. Even though they compete with each other to some degree, all can help attract repeat business to the area.

Diplomacy

14. RECOMMENDATION: The metropolitan region should undertake a concerted campaign to establish more foreign consulates (full or honorary) and trade offices here, with a goal of at least doubling the number of consulates by the year 2000. Once the new international conference center is completed at the waterfront, the area's congressional delegation should assist local officials in attracting high-level international diplomatic "summits" and other meetings.

In the diplomatic arena, the Consular Corps of Seattle, representing 35 foreign countries, is an integral part of the region's business and cultural community. Nine nations have career consuls general here, while the rest have honorary consuls. The newest, the Consulate of Hungary, was announced at Discovery Institute's International Seattle conference in May 1993. The Consulate General of Russia was officially established in December 1992. The Phillipine government said in early 1993 that it would close its Seattle consulate, and 11 other diplomatic posts worldwide, but an effort is underway, led by Secretary of State Ralph Munro and members of the local Filipino community, to keep the consulate here.

In comparison to Seattle's 35 consulates, Los

Angeles has 75 consulates, San Francisco 65, San Diego 35, and Vancouver, B.C., 46. In the East., New York has 87, Houston 56, Atlanta 46 and Boston 34. In addition to consulates, the governments of Canada and Denmark have Trade Commissions here, and there is a Kobe Trade Information Office. In February 1993, however, the government of Mexico announced that it would close its trade office here, as well as those in several

Sister Cities tend to have a life of their own, a kind of bureaucratic immortality.

other nations, because of budgetary problems.

The entire region could benefit from more consulates and trade offices, which are one of the best indices of a city's international activity and stature. The Trade Development Alliance of Greater Seattle should lead this effort, functioning as a kind of "secretariat" for this campaign. A public-private non-profit organization should be created to help attract more consulates. Through it, individuals or corporations could make tax-exempt contributions of funds, space, equipment or services. Washington State's Congressional delegation should make sure that the U.S. State Department is sympathetic and helpful, by taking consistent steps to monitor the process and ensure the department's support.

This effort might focus initially on Central European countries and the former Soviet republics of the Commonwealth of Independent States, where the Seattle area has been developing close relationships for two decades. It was a highly significant development when Seattle became the site of a new Russian consulate. In return, the United States is establishing a new American consulate in Vladivostok, in the Russian Far East, and a consulate in St. Petersburg.

Seattle should soon be the best equipped city in the West to attract high-level diplomatic meetings, thanks to its new Port-sponsored conference center.

Local officials should stimulate federal cooperation to see that Seattle is considered for important international gatherings sponsored by the United States.

Sister Cities

15. RECOMMENDATION: Metropolitan Seattle-area Sister City Committees should all be rechartered, based on new criteria for membership and activities. Inactive committees probably should be disbanded.

Seattle may not lead in consulates and trade offices, but it now has 20 Sister Cities, more than any other American city. In 1991-92 alone, Seattle added five: Kaohsiung, Taiwan; Pecs, Hungary; Perugia, Italy; Surabaya, Indonesia; and Cebu, Philippines. And a 20th—Gdynia, Poland—was approved in 1993.

The most active Sister City relationships include those with Kobe, Japan; Tashkent, Uzbekistan; Bergen, Norway; Nantes, France; Mazatlan, Mexico; Christchurch, New Zealand; and Chongqing, China. Some Sister City committees—including Tashkent, Kobe, and Christchurch—regularly publish attractive newsletters. Seattle and Bergen have a well-established sister school relationship, and an exchange program between the University of Washington's Engineering Department and the University of Bergen has blossomed over the years. There is an active teacher-exchange program with Chongqing, China.

Among other cities in the metropolitan region, Tacoma has 5 Sister Cities, Bellevue 3, Everett 3, Kent 2, and Auburn, Edmonds, Issaquah, Renton, and Tukwila one each.

However, Sister Cities tend to have a life of their own, or one might say, an existence after life—a kind of bureaucratic immortality. Once they're born, there's no end to them—even if they cease to be active and meaningful relationships. The fact that Seattle now has more Sister Cities than any other U.S. city may either be seen as something to boast about, or as a cause for embarrassment. In some cases, Sister Cities are artificial relationships and have little geographic, cultural or political justification. While some of those mentioned above are still active and vital, others—such as Limbe,

Cameroon; Reykjavik, Iceland; and Mombasa, Kenya—are already virtually defunct.

It's time for a thorough review of all Sister City relationships, and a housecleaning if necessary. They should be refocused on helping any school, neighborhood group, business, service club or other organization seeking to establish relationships with a "sister" group overseas. Finally, they should be depoliticized so they're not vehicles for ideological activism or opposition to U.S. foreign policy.

Media

16. RECOMMENDATION: The metropolitan region's news media—both print and broadcast—should give higher priority to international news coverage, and particularly pay more attention to regional events and developments with international implications.

To their credit, the local media have made great

More can be done by all the local media to increase and improve their international coverage.

improvements in international coverage and awareness in recent years. Both Seattle daily newspapers, for example, have had full-time Pacific Rim reporters for the past few years. Both have identified international activity as an important component of regional progress which they have pledged to promote—*The Seattle Times* did so in the Peirce Report that it published in 1989, and the *Post-Intelligencer* in its "P-I Agenda" which it regularly publishes on the editorial page. The newspapers in Tacoma, Bellevue and Everett also have improved their international coverage. The *Seattle Weekly* offers only occasional, but often excellent, international pieces. The *Puget Sound Business Journal* is

consistently informative on international topics.

Local broadcast outlets have made similar innovations: KING, KIRO and KOMO television stations all have sent crews overseas on an increasingly frequent basis in recent years. KIRO radio has done the same, including some innovative broadcasts from Japan and the Soviet Union. And in the public-television realm, KCTS-9 has been a leader in international ventures, such as its cross-border programming and fund-raising activities in British Columbia, where it has many loyal viewers. Also, the station's "Asia Today" program and others have been ground-breaking and excellent.

Still, more can be done by all the local media to increase and improve their international coverage, even in times of tight budgets. Some suggestions:

❑ The local media should make better use of local foreign-policy experts. There are many people in this community—college professors, business executives, retired diplomats and others—who have enormous expertise in international affairs but are seldom consulted by the local media. The print and broadcast media should cultivate better relationships with these individuals, and call upon them for commentary and perspective when major news events occur in particular places around the world.

❑ The local papers might consider assembling a "board of contributors" who would write regular op-ed pieces on international topics. KCTS-9 might produce a weekly program on international affairs, using local experts and visiting international figures in a Q-&-A roundtable format.

❑ Local media should provide better coverage of international conferences and meetings on foreign affairs that take place here, which too often are given short shrift or are simply ignored. For example, the North American Free Trade Agreement talks held here in August 1991 did not attract the kind of coverage they deserved. And in October 1992, a press conference called to announce federal funding for a new Cascadia Corridor Commission was cancelled when no one from the media even showed up. Important international events that take place here deserve better coverage. If the organizers of such events receive no coverage, they won't want to come back. They'll hold their conferences in Washington, D.C., Los Angeles or other places where they will draw attention.

❑ Regional media should operate more exchange programs in which local and foreign journalists spend time at each others' publications or broadcast stations. That would help members of the media gain a broader and deeper perspective on international affairs. They could then do a better job of educating the public on what international trade, tourism and other contacts do for the city and region economically, culturally, and politically.

❑ Local radio and TV stations and cable companies should explore opportunities for more local programming in foreign languages, including news, special events, movies, etc. If subtitled, they would attract a wider audience. How about running a Japanese soap opera, which would help us learn about the culture as well as learn the language? Why not offer the BBC on a local cable channel? How about an entire Russian- or Chinese-language channel?

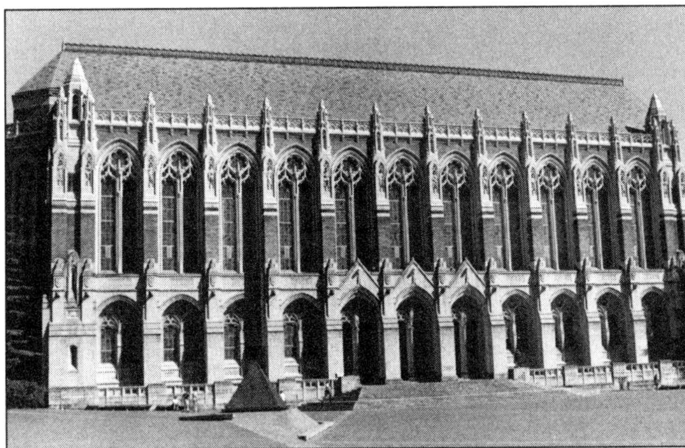

Suzzallo Library, University of Washington

Higher Education

17. RECOMMENDATION: Metropolitan Seattle's corporate community should develop a long-range funding plan for the Center for International Business Education and Research (CIBER) at the U.W. Business School. An academically competitive international business school will facilitate a competitive strategy for our region, and local corporations will benefit.

The U.W. Business School has not always strongly emphasized international business, but that has, of necessity, begun to change. Forward-looking faculty and staff of the school have realized that all students must be better prepared to function in what has become a true global economy. To that end, a Center for International Business and Research (CIBER) was established in 1990, to promote several innovative programs and courses, including:

❑ The International Management Fellows Program, a graduate-level certificate program within the U.W.'s regular Master of Business Administration (MBA) program. It is a two-year program that includes advanced language study, in-depth area study, and an overseas business internship. It offers four language tracks: Chinese, German, Japanese and Spanish. Currently 12 students are enrolled, but the goal is to have 10 students in each track, for a total of 40 each year.

❑ Certificate of International Studies in Business, an undergraduate program that also offers different language tracks. Currently 27 undergraduates are enrolled, with a goal of 70 students each year.

❑ International Business Association, a club whose goal is to let more MBA students have direct contact with CIBER and the chance to take part in a speaker series and other activities. CIBER-organized courses are open to any student at the U.W. A proposal has been made to involve the Jackson School of International Studies and other schools in the College of Arts and Sciences more closely in CIBER's efforts. CIBER's budget is now split about 50-50 between a $285,000 grant from the U.S. Department of Education, matched by about $294,000 in university and private funds, including a contribution from the Bank of Tokyo. But there is no guarantee the federal grant will be extended, and the program clearly deserves more support from the region's corporate community.

18. RECOMMENDATION: The University of Washington, and other regional universities and colleges, should seek to increase the number of students they send to study abroad to at least match the number of international students who come to study here. In addition, they should encourage more faculty participation in exchange programs. Stronger support for grant development

would help pay for the increase.

The June 1991 Foreign Study Office report noted a severe imbalance between the number of U.W. students studying abroad and number of foreign students coming to the U.W. In a typical academic year, for instance, about 450 U.W. undergraduates and 100 graduate students study abroad, representing about 1.5 percent of total enrollment of some 35,000 students. Meanwhile, in 1991-92, 1,837 international students came to the U.W. campus to study, representing more than 5 percent of enrollment. Moreover, over 90 percent of U.W. students who go abroad study in Europe, while 90 percent of the foreign students coming here are from Asia.

Still, the number of U.W. students going abroad has steadily increased since the mid-1980s, except for a slight drop in the 1990-91 school year that was attributed to the Gulf War. In the spring term of 1986, for example, only 104 students studied abroad. In the spring of 1992, the number had more than doubled to 215 (although spring is traditionally the most popular quarter for foreign study).

There needs to be an expansion of exchange programs and increased funding for student participants. Research or study abroad is relatively inexpensive, but has enormous long-term paybacks. The more exchanges, the better. The fact that more than three times as many foreign students come here as U.W. students go abroad is a telling commentary.

The lack of balance in U.W. student participation also should be addressed. Currently, the majority of U.W. participants are white females who study in Western Europe. The ethnic and gender base of participants should be expanded, as well as the geographic distribution of programs and exchanges. For example, U.W. exchanges in Asia are limited and in Africa, virtually nonexistent.

Educators and administrators at other local universities and community colleges also report that foreign-study programs have gained in popularity over the past decade. Examples:

❑ North Seattle Community College has had Study Abroad since the 1970s, but interest has increased greatly over the last few years and enthusiasm has grown among faculty and students.

❑ Seattle Pacific University offers a variety of Study Abroad programs and sends about 65 students overseas each year, including 25 who participate in an annual fall European Quarter.

❑ Seattle University's International Studies Office was established in 1990, and interest has risen steadily in Study Abroad programs. In the 1989-90 school year, for example, 38 Seattle University students went abroad; in 1991-92, the number climbed to 63.

As for faculty exchanges, travel and research abroad can give faculty members a broader global outlook and help achieve the overall goal of internationalizing the classroom. So can bringing more international faculty here. Regional academic administrations should recognize those facts and take steps to significantly increase faculty-exchange programs. The issue of how participation in international activities affects faculty members in terms of tenure also must be addressed. They should certainly not be penalized; on the contrary, they should be rewarded for increasing their international expertise.

Many U.W. professors go overseas each year and numerous foreign professors and scholars come to the Seattle campus. However, there is no centralized coordination or monitoring of this activity, and thus is it difficult to collect accurate information. No one knows the exact number of U.W. professors who are overseas at any given time. These exchanges are most often the result of individual faculty members' contacts overseas. Still, there is a need for a computerized data base to keep track of these exchanges.

During any recent year, about 1,000 foreign scholars (instructors and researchers) are at the U.W. for periods of time ranging from a single quarter to several years. They are funded from various sources, including government, private, personal or U.W. support. A large percentage (44 percent in 1990) are from Asia. Their primary fields of research are the sciences, engineering and medicine.

As for other colleges and universities in the metropolitan Seattle area, there are also many exchanges going on, but little coordination or monitoring of this activity. At Seattle University, for instance, exchanges are handled on a departmental basis rather than by the central administration. In spring quarter of 1992, for example, there were two visiting professors—one from Sweden and one from England—and two SU professors with plans to go abroad—one to Belgium and one to Czechoslovakia. Similarly, Seattle Pacific University in 1992 had four temporary foreign faculty members—two from India, one from Canada and one from New Zealand. North Seattle Community College exchanges two instructors each year, to Poland and Taiwan, and has plans for similar swaps in Japan and China.

> 19. RECOMMENDATION: Metropolitan Seattle's community colleges and private colleges and universities also must continue to improve their international education programs. It would be helpful if the many calls for "multiculturalism" were to focus less on contemporary cultural perceptions and delve more deeply and positively into the cultural heritage of various countries— their history, philosophy, religion, art and economics.

New efforts are being made throughout the higher-education community in metropolitan Seattle to include international issues and dimensions in the curriculum. Two trends are especially praiseworthy: One is the general strategy of internationalizing the curriculum, which includes incorporating international aspects into courses in various fields of study. The other is adding courses that deal with international affairs specifically, or introducing a new international studies major altogether.

❏ Seattle University, for example, started an international studies major in 1990 as part of its liberal-arts program. Since its inception, the number of students participating has increased dramatically: from only 4 in the summer of 1990 to 45 in the winter of 1992.

❏ Edmonds Community College also has extensive efforts underway to increase global awareness. Six years ago, the school received a federal Title III grant from the U.S. Department of Education to internationalize the entire curriculum.

❏ International Programs at Bellevue Community College began as an institute to provide English language training to university-bound foreign students in the early 1980s. Since then it has grown in size and scope and now provides language, international business, market economics and other academic training to students and business people from throughout the world.

Youth who have had some experience abroad are clearly more likely as adults to pursue occupations in international affairs.

❏ The International Trade Institute at North Seattle Community College offers an extensive array of practical, nuts-and-bolts classes and professional training in international commerce and trade. Its International Trade Certificate Program helps small-business owners, employees and entrepreneurs interested in competing effectively in the international marketplace. Founded in 1987 with 300 students, the Institute grew to 920 participants in 1989, then began a decline as advertising and promotion were reduced and the program was cut back from four quarters to only two quarters. A total of 537 students were enrolled in 1992.

At North Seattle Community College, there is a commendable effort to expand international programs. Peter Ku, NSCC's president, is leading an innovative program to create a residential international education center. NSCC's International Education Advisory Committee completed a master plan that aims to integrate intercultural perspectives into the curriculum through special courses, lectures and assignments with global themes. "International Education at NSCC: A Plan for the 1990s" contains a valuable set of recommendations that could be applied to all the region's community colleges, including: Developing international curriculum guidelines to encourage faculty to include global issues in their courses; internationalizing the curriculum through specially designed courses and lectures or assignments on global themes; continuing to offer foreign languages, English as a Second Language, and bilingual programs; encouraging international travel by faculty and staff, and exchanging more faculty with institutions abroad; enrolling more international students (up to 2 percent of the student body), and forming partnerships with colleges in other countries to provide exchanges for faculty and students; and offering annual lecture series on international issues.

Another promising development is a bill passed by the 1993 Legislature to establish a Washington State Task Force on International Education, under the Higher Education Coordinating Board. In addition, representatives of the state's six four-year universities and the community colleges have been meeting to discuss cooperative international programs to save costs, which should be strongly encouraged by the HEC Board.

Continuing Education

20. RECOMMENDATION: The region's institutions of higher education and the nonprofit international organizations should develop a coordinated strategy to maximize continuing-education opportunities for adults in various aspects of internationalism, and produce a comprehensive publication describing available programs and activities.

This area already offers many opportunities for learning foreign languages, studying international affairs, and appreciating other cultures. There is the University of Washington's excellent evening lecture series and travel program, run through Spectrum, and a nationally renowned intensive Russian-study summer program. The World Affairs Council sponsors a steady stream of luncheons, dinners and other events with notable international leaders. The Washington Council on International Trade, Japan America Society, World Trade Club and other groups have regular guest lectures, seminars, conferences

and cultural events. And language classes are offered by a host of organizations, public and private.

The international awareness of an informed public is itself a contribution to the competitiveness of the region in global affairs. There should be a concerted effort to encourage all programs that heighten public awareness through sustained efforts in international education such as those mentioned above. The goal should be to make internationalism part of the civic spirit and self-image in metropolitan

> *Ideally, more teachers should have the opportunity to travel or live abroad, so they can bring broader international perspectives into their classrooms.*

Seattle, much like Vancouver, B.C., which clearly takes pride in and actively promotes its international cosmopolitanism.

In addition, the region should encourage more people-to-people exchanges and home-stay programs for students and adults, whether tourists, businesspeople, government officials or others. Such experiences not only can increase understanding and goodwill, but also may lead to trade, investment or other business deals in the long run. The region also should provide more support for the World Affairs Council's International Visitors Program, which offers such opportunities and contacts. Local businesses could help advertise it, and perhaps solicit their employees and customers to become involved in the program.

Foreign tours are a popular international activity sponsored by many of the region's educational institutions. Bellevue Community College, as part of International Programs, offers tours to foreign destinations to students, faculty and the public. Edmonds Community College has organized tours to China. North Seattle Community College devises travel seminars to enhance global awareness, which culminate in overseas tours.

These activities are all praiseworthy, but better coordination and wide distribution of a comprehensive brochure or newsletter describing all available programs would build a larger constituency in the region for internationalism. Perhaps the newly formed cooperative group of community college and university representatives could take on this task.

K-12 Education

21. RECOMMENDATION: The region's schools should double the number of students who experience an international trip, a junior-year abroad program, or (at the very least) host foreign visitors here by the year 2000. In addition, metropolitan-area school districts, businesses and foundations should increase support for travel abroad and training sessions in internationalism for elementary and secondary-school teachers.

Travel abroad can be an enlightening experience, the kind that not only opens the door of international understanding for youth, but leads them confidently through it. Youth who have some experience abroad are clearly more likely as adults to pursue occupations in international affairs. If this region wants to be a leader in international trade and related fields, it should lead the United States in participation in student-exchange programs. All students who aspire to real fluency in a foreign language, especially, should have the opportunity to spend at least a summer, and preferably a year, abroad.

In order for this to happen, the metropolitan region's school district supervisors, teachers, counselors, parents and others should not only support increased language instruction, but should call on local businesses and civic groups to provide funds. For example, companies could give foreign-language scholarships to students for study abroad, or help sponsor total-immersion summer schools for intensive language and culture training. The Japan America Society's summer camp near Puyallup is an excellent model for such programs.

In a related issue, it's worth noting that actual experience abroad, and especially time spent living overseas, is what solidifies the future benefits of language instruction and gives students a superior understanding of other societies. There's nothing like living in another country to learn the bad as well as the good aspects of a foreign culture, and to better appreciate and understand one's own culture. As Washington Irving once said: "No one knows his own country until he's lived in another." Living abroad can be a great cure for young Americans' trendy and simplistic anti-Americanism, as well.

However, another disturbing indication of

A new International High School would be an enormously valuable addition to the local educational scene, and give serious students of internationalism a unique choice.

lukewarm interest in international affairs is the lack of applicants for foreign-exchange programs from at least some area high schools. For example, the Bellevue Rotary Club's youth exchange committee reported that applicants for foreign study fellowships and summer exchanges actually dropped to half the number applying 10 years ago. Only 18 students applied for 40 positions available in the 1992-93 school year. American Field Service applications in the Seattle region have declined in recent years as well.

Students and counselors offer a variety of reasons why the interest in exchange programs is low: the perception that Americans do not need to know other languages to succeed, while English is a key to international success; the high cost of foreign travel and exchange programs; the fear of intimidation that might come from studying in a foreign culture;

family concerns that dissuade students from living abroad for a full year before leaving home for college or a job; concerns about being "out of synch" with classmates; and an attitude that might be characterized as "Why study abroad when America is the envy of the world?" Still, there are good responses for most of these concerns, including such benefits of foreign-exchange programs as wider global perspective, greater self-confidence, improved language competence, greater college competitiveness, enhanced career opportunities, broader political insights, making new friends and simply having fun. These need to be better explained by parents, teachers, counselors and the media.

One of the best ways to increase interest and excitement in internationalism among students is to expose them to teachers who are knowledgeable and enthusiastic about global issues and connections. Ideally, more teachers should have the opportunity to travel or live abroad, so they can bring broader international perspectives into their classrooms. Alternatively, they can attend some of the special training sessions that are already available in the region—and which should be expanded to accommodate more teachers.

Currently, interest in foreign-exchange programs for teachers is strong but funding is limited. In the summer of 1992, the University of Washington's Jackson School of International Studies and the state Office of Superintendent of Public Instruction took 12 social-studies teachers to Japan. OSPI cosponsors teacher exchanges with Japan, Australia and Denmark, and provides grants for some electronic linkages for teachers and students of Spanish.

The Jackson School's Outreach Program, which runs summer training classes for K-12 teachers in international studies, is another effort worthy of more support. The School offers a month-long summer course for teachers, "Perspectives on Teaching About International Studies," which always fills up. It also offers weekend workshops for teachers focusing on specific countries or world issues. The Washington Council on International Trade's annual summer training seminar for high-school teachers, which gives 30 to 40 teachers an intensive program in international trade, is another excellent model

that deserves more support and expansion.

> *Regional schools should do everything possible to encourage more innovative use of computer technology and software for international education.*

22. RECOMMENDATION: A special study commission should be formed to reexamine the idea of establishing a new International High School somewhere in the metropolitan region. Conversion of an existing public or private school to an international format might offer the soundest financial way to develop this concept.

A new International High School would be an enormously valuable addition to the local educational scene, and give serious students of internationalism a unique choice. For those students who are interested at an early age in international careers, there should be opportunities to study foreign languages and an international curriculum more intensively than in other schools. There also should be courses focusing on international business and global competitiveness, which are widely available in international schools in Japan, Germany, Holland and other nations where internationalism is emphasized early.

While it is true that internationalism should be a larger part of every school's curriculum, an International High School would play a special role. The prospect of an International High School was studied at length in the 1980s, but the idea ultimately was abandoned. It is time to revive the notion and take a thorough look at its feasibility.

To examine this possibility, a Special Study Commission should be formed to look at how other communities have successfully established International Schools. They should visit several such schools in the United States, Europe and Asia to gather ideas. One possible model: Indianapolis, where a commission was formed to establish an international school and recently hired a headmaster.

Such a school could teach languages such as Arabic, Thai and Swahili, that are not taught at any other area schools. It could have outside experts such as retired international business executives and citizens of other countries who are temporarily residing here available to augment its faculty. It also should offer the International Baccalaureate Degree. Locally, only Foss High School in Tacoma and Mount Rainier High School in Burien offer the International Baccalaureate, an intensive academic program originally developed by Oxford University that gives 11th and 12th grade students a basic curriculum competitive with the world's best secondary schools. More than 40 countries accept the International Baccalaureate in lieu of college-entrance exams.

While several approaches are possible, it is most likely that such a school would be private rather than public. This does not necessarily mean that other efforts such as the International Magnet Program at Cleveland High School in Seattle should be abandoned—although if it is to succeed it needs far more support and resources, including the

Seattle's rich ethnic heritage can increase this area's global appeal.

addition of Horizon and Advanced Placement Programs to attract more dedicated students.

The Bellevue International Middle School, which started in the fall of 1991 for sixth- and seventh-graders, is another public-system model that deserves continued support. It was a great success in its first year, earning enthusiastic response among students, faculty, parents and the community by offering a global perspective and relating subject matter to world events, cultures and problems. It also stresses integrating international elements into core subjects such as math, science and social studies. The school received 150 applications for the only 70 slots it had open for the current school year. The response in Bellevue is strong evidence that this region could

support a new International High School.

In addition, all regional schools should take maximum advantage of advances in computer technology and software for international education. The use of more electronic computer networks to link with other schools worldwide can be a tremendously stimulating experience for students. Such linkages with students in Japan, the former U.S.S.R., the Middle East, Scandinavia and other places have already proved highly popular and have exposed students to their peers in a unique way. Regional schools should do everything possible to encourage more innovative use of computer technology, such as encouraging small groups of schools around the world to work together on joint projects.

Some schools and districts in this region have been innovators in using computer networks to establish connections with other schools around the world. Foster High School in Tukwila is a notable example, as is the South Kitsap School District. They should be considered models for similar programs and efforts throughout the region.

Another especially innovative program is underway in the Issaquah School District, where the Technology Information Project (TIP) has set a goal of installing a district-wide computer network, largely designed by students themselves. It eventually will connect all classrooms and offices in 17 schools with a local area network (LAN), using primarily Microsoft software. The system will be unique in the United States and has the potential of linking the schools into an international telecommunications network including worldwide electronic mail.

Ethnic Heritage

23. RECOMMENDATION: The region should undertake a coordinated strategy to showcase metropolitan Seattle's rich ethnic heritage as a way to increase this area's global appeal.

Although this region—once known as the home of "trees and Swedes"—has not historically been famous for its diversity, metropolitan Seattle actually has a fairly varied ethnic population. Granted, the Asian-American, African-American, Native American and other ethnic populations are relatively small compared to those in some other cities, but each has unique strengths and rich traditions. Community resources—tax revenues, foundation grants, private donations, etc.—are devoted now to providing basic social services to several of these communities, and helping make troubled ethnic neighborhoods more self-sufficient. However, part of that effort surely should consist of programs to help these communities develop and promote their own cultural heritage in a way that would be appealing and attractive, as well as educational, to domestic and international tourists.

This is not to suggest patronizing or spotlighting these communities for sheer entertainment value. Rather, it would entail helping them express pride in their culture, traditions and accomplishments and explaining those features to outsiders. For example, the Wing Luke Museum in the International District hosted a remarkable collection of photographs and memorabilia from the World War II years of Japanese internment, which did much to educate the general public on that unfortunate chapter in U.S. history and rekindle pride among Japanese-Americans. The collection is of such a quality that it should be put on permanent display somewhere in the community.

Seattle's International District, long known as "Chinatown," is probably more diverse than some other American cities' so-called "Chinatowns" because of its rich mix of cultures, including Chinese, Japanese, Filipino, Taiwanese, Vietnamese, Cambodian, Thai, Laotian, Korean, Samoan and others. Overall, Washington State has the third-largest concentration of Southeast Asians in the U.S., behind only California and Texas. Again, that is a strength which should not only be preserved, but promoted. The region's Asian-American community is a great and growing asset, whose bicultural population is an excellent bridge to the Pacific Rim.

The International District is a prime resource for local residents and for international tourists, yet it is not well advertised or marketed by the city or other tourist-promotion agencies. A new Asian Cultural Center, as has been proposed for the International District, would be an invaluable addition. If it is financed adequately and planned carefully, it could be a place where generations of Seattle-area citizens, as well as national and international tourists of all races, learn regional history with a stress on the role of Asian-Americans. It could anchor the future of the International District with a major attraction: a historical and cultural center that would be a site for art, music, drama, exhibits and other activities.

Similarly, the Daybreak Star Indian Cultural Center at Discovery Park needs to be more broadly developed and supported as a prime cultural attraction. It is a good example of an admirable effort to build a cultural center with modest resources, but it is not nearly what this region deserves in terms of a showcase for our Native American heritage. Indian history and tradition have an enormous claim on our culture, and are important to the regional psyche—yet have been sadly neglected. Daybreak Star needs and deserves major upgrading and permanent financial support. The recent proposal for a $25 million Peoples Lodge expansion should be taken up as a challenge for the whole region, which is home to more Native Americans than is any other community in the Northwest quarter of America. Of course, Daybreak Star needs to be sensitively integrated into Discovery Park. However, it should not be forgotten that the park design was, from its inception, meant to include a major Indian cultural center for the region. Also, it needs to be recognized that the center can have considerable economic impact. Native American culture is far more appealing to international tourists than is commonly known. Yet other parts of the Pacific Northwest, most notably Vancouver, B.C., preserve and present their Native American cultural assets much more effectively than we do, and to their distinct advantages.

In addition, the metropolitan region must do a better job of supporting its African American culture and community, which can be a great asset in terms of this area's international image and appeal. The region's black population is relatively small compared to some other major American cities, but it has a number of excellent, active organizations that sponsor vibrant and popular cultural events. Black History Month and Festival Sundiata in February, and the Black Community Festival and Soul Festival in July, should be more widely promoted and marketed to local residents and tourists alike. The Seattle Art Museum has one of the world's best collections of African art, and it was spotlighted in a spectacular opening in January 1992 in which the region's African American community was deeply involved. A special newspaper tabloid section in the *Seattle Post-Intelligencer* did much to encourage young people's interest in the African heritage. The region should continue to look for similarly innovative ways to help the African American community celebrate its great contributions to this area's cultural diversity.

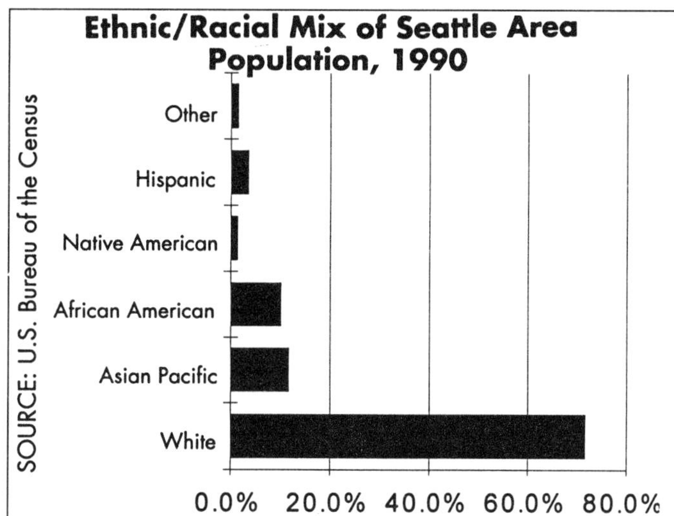

And of course, the region's European-American ethnic groups are important to this community's heritage as well, and must not be overlooked. Paying for ethnic cultural improvements of the kind advocated here will be easier if the strategy of global competitiveness is broadly adopted—the theme of our study.

Nonprofit Groups

24. RECOMMENDATION: A consortium of local organizations should undertake the task of compiling a comprehensive list and description of all the nonprofit groups in this region that are active in international affairs, to serve as a resource for those interested in the field.

Metropolitan Seattle certainly does not suffer from a shortage of groups interested in international affairs. In fact, there are so many of them it is difficult to keep track, and confusing for anyone new to the area to get a good sense of the players in the field. That's why a good, updated guide to these groups would be an invaluable resource.

"Tools of the Trade," published by the Trade Development Alliance and the Washington Council on International Trade, is excellent as far as it goes. But it is by no means comprehensive and is short on detail about many groups. The International Resource Center Directory is a comprehensive listing of groups statewide that are involved in international affairs, but it also lacks detail and could be more attractively packaged.

"Washington's Window on the World," published in 1982 by the World Without War Council, is a good model of what's needed, but is now badly out of date. More recent models are "Assembling the Mosaic: A Guide to the World Affairs Field in Chicago," published in 1991, and "Americans & World Affairs," a guide to the organizations and institutions in Northern California, published in 1988, both also done by regional World Without War Councils.

Local organizations, foundations and corporations could help underwrite the costs of compiling and publishing such a guide to the metropolitan Seattle area. It also could be made available on electronic media, which would facilitate the regular updating that would no doubt be necessary, since there is so much turnover in this field. This effort could be led by the restructured metropolitan-area foreign office described in this report's first recommendation.

25. RECOMMENDATION: The metropolitan region's business, government and nonprofit leaders should set a goal of having one or more major international foundations locate here.

A major world-class foundation can be an enormous resource for a metropolitan region—and this area lacks one. Consider what the Lilly Endowment has done for Indianapolis, and the Northwest Area Foundation for Minneapolis. Such a foundation here could gain an international reputation by funding major research, sending

Seattle-area people worldwide to do studies, bringing international scholars here to work or study, and generally enhancing the status of this region as a world leader in internationalism.

Related to this recommendation, the region should strive to create a climate among the public and the media that gives more credit to existing local foundations that generously support worthy causes. They deserve much more recognition as a matter of decency, of course, but also as a practical consideration: If foundations receive wider appreciation, they are likely to support more worthwhile activities. Such local groups as the Seattle Foundation, Weyerhaeuser Foundation, Paccar Foundation, Henry M. Jackson Foundation and others play invaluable philanthropic roles in our community. Public praise is a powerful motivator, and local foundations deserve more of it.

Likewise, the leadership of the metropolitan region should give more recognition to individuals who give their money to worthy causes. In cities where largesse is viewed as an act of civic worth, people are more inclined to give. Philanthropy is a genuine statement of optimism in one's community, and special praise should be given to those who donate their money voluntarily. Sometimes such praise is forthcoming here, as when the Bullitt Foundation was established with proceeds from the sale of KING-TV. But in other cases, acts of philanthropy are largely ignored. That must change. Public recognition from political, media and business leaders can help—and make it more likely that a major international foundation may someday locate here.

One encouraging effort is the Pacific Northwest Grantmakers Forum, an association of philanthropic groups in the five Pacific Northwest states. It works to promote more effective grantmaking through information exchange, conferences and workshops. However, of the Forum's 90-plus members, only six fund international programs.

> **26. RECOMMENDATION:** The metropolitan region's leaders should set a goal of having a major international agency and/or non-profit institution locate here.

The presence of major international agencies makes an enormous contribution to any community's worldwide reputation. Consider Vienna, site of numerous United Nations organizations, or Brussels and Strasbourg, where different branches of the European Community are headquartered. Metropolitan Seattle should strive to attract an international institution. Possibilities might be a new United Nations agency or a new International Climate Prediction Center. Or we could encourage existing agencies, such as the U.N. Environment Programme, to have part of their staffs spend summers here.

Efforts also should be made to persuade major private non-profit international organizations to put their headquarters or regional offices in this area. About 400 such groups exist in the U.S., focusing on global education, environment, student exchange, relief and development, and other issues. If we attract just one major group, that would make us a focal point and help to draw others. To that end, the region should provide more incentives for nonprofit groups to relocate here— low-priced real estate, office space, tax incentives, and other special arrangements.

It can be done: In September 1992, CARE USA, after a year-long search, decided to relocate its headquarters from New York City to Atlanta. Atlanta was selected over other cities because it offered CARE a fully renovated downtown building for office space.

Downtown Seattle waterfront

In addition, the Robert Woodruff Foundation of Atlanta committed several million dollars for relocation and related expenses. CARE officials said that among their objectives in moving were lower operating costs, greater productivity, and enhanced ability to attract overseas staff. If Atlanta could provide all those things, why not Seattle?

In Indianapolis, efforts by the Lilly Endowment, working in concert with business and government leaders, have succeeded in attracting several international offices of non-profit organizations to that city.

Arts/Culture

27. RECOMMENDATION: The metropolitan Seattle area should establish an annual month-long International Summer Arts Festival, modeled after the Goodwill Arts Festival, to bring world-renowned musicians, dancers, artists, actors, authors and others here for a series of events that would include numerous world premiers and original works. Pooling of disparate current international arts activities could help make such a goal financially feasible.

The draft version of this report recommended a summer-long arts festival, but many members of the local arts community said that was overly ambitious, so we instead suggest a month-long annual festival sometime between the Northwest Folklife Festival on Memorial Day Weekend and Bumbershoot on Labor Day Weekend. The festival should build on what we already have, but add or reschedule other events as needed. This would provide a focus to the summer and, if well planned and executed, offer a West Coast version of the Spoleto Festival in Charleston, South Carolina.

Granted, the debate over how best to coordinate and market arts and cultural events in this region has gone on for decades. Some have suggested promoting this area as a "Festival City," where something is happening during all months of the year. But that seems too diffuse and it doesn't stress quality, which is vital to such an undertaking. Also, let's face it, the summer months are the best time to attract visitors, not to mention providing events for local residents to enjoy. It may be desirable to give

each summer a different international theme, just as the Goodwill Arts Festival focused on Russian culture—with the Art Treasures of Moscow, the Bolshoi Ballet, the opera production of "War and Peace," and the Sovremenik Theater's Russian-language production of "Into the Whirlwind" at Intiman. The events would combine novelty and tradition, with the overall theme of international

Seattle Art Museum

understanding and appreciation for art and culture. There would be many important openings, for which tickets could be sold at a premium, providing increased revenues and the kind of special atmosphere that many Seattle-area residents saw during the Goodwill Arts Festival—a heady, inspiring experience that had seldom before been felt in this community.

Such a festival could be culturally enriching for local citizens and tremendously attractive to domestic and international tourists. Some have suggested that such an ambitious festival be held only every few years, or every other year. But it must be annual to work; otherwise, people tend to become confused as to which year the festival is on and find it difficult to make plans in advance. An annual festival, being predictable, is more likely to become ingrained in people's minds. Plus, visitors could count on finding something of interest if they came to Seattle during the summer—just as one can always count on finding first-class events during Spoleto, or during summers in Salzburg, or, closer to home, during the Oregon

Shakespearean Festival. The Seattle Opera's past productions of Wagner's "The Ring" cycle, which won worldwide acclaim and attracted visitors from many countries, are another example of what a first-rate cultural event can do for a city.

One promising recent development: A Seattle International Music Festival was inaugurated in August 1993 under the direction of Dmitry Sitkovetsky. Formerly the Santa Fe Chamber Music Festival, the new group will range from solo performances to full orchestras. In 1994, it will begin featuring the New European Strings, a 20-piece ensemble whose members are mostly Europeans or Russian emigres. The initial season was considered a great artistic and commercial success; the Seattle International Music Festival could well become the prestigious festival we are advocating.

A thorough, excellent study, "Encore!?—Exploring the Options of an International Arts Festival," was prepared in September 1991 for One Reel, Seattle's premier arts-promotion company, by The Collins Group, a Seattle consulting firm. The study found: 1) almost unanimous praise for the 1990 Goodwill Arts Festival; 2) a reluctance to take on the challenge of a future International Arts Festival, and 3) a sense that given the right conditions, such a festival could be successfully staged. The study's final conclusion was: "If a compelling theme, exciting project, clear leadership, and external financial support were present, there would be participation by arts organizations and support forthcoming by corporate, private and governmental entities." The study's findings and conclusions are still valid, but it's time to reassess the reluctance and take on the challenge.

Museums

28. RECOMMENDATION: The metropolitan region's historical and cultural museums should undertake a joint marketing and promotion effort to better present themselves to international visitors.

This area's historical museums constitute a large part of the distinctive culture of the region which we wish to display to the rest of the world. Our museum message is diffuse today, however. The Klondike Gold Rush National Historical Park on Occidental Square, the Museum of History and Industry in the Montlake neighborhood of Seattle, the Burke Memorial Washington State Museum on the University of Washington Campus, the Nordic Heritage Museum in Ballard, and the Washington State Historical Museum in Tacoma are all admirable institutions, with good collections, but what they have on display (and even where they are located) is often unknown to many local residents. Imagine the difficulty, then, that international tourists have in identifying and visiting these museums!

What is needed is a joint promotional package—probably consisting of a new brochure or small guidebook, some coordinated campaigns or events, a packaged tour, and perhaps even a joint admission ticket—that would raise the profile of these institutions. They could be promoted together with the Seattle Art Museum, the Daybreak Star Indian Cultural Center, and even the Tillicum Village salmon barbecue, as a way to gain deeper understanding of Pacific Northwest history and culture. This region's Native American and pioneer past, along with the development of the logging, fishing, and mining industries, are all things that international visitors are interested in and that are distinctive. For those who are interested, side tours to Eastern Washington to see rodeos, Indian festivals, or to stay in dude ranches, could be offered in the promotional material as well.

The idea here is that our history and culture are among the best things we have to offer to visitors, along with our fabulous flora and fauna, and these things should be better promoted as unique and accessible to those who may come from around the world to see them. Actually, this approach could be extended to include all the region's museums. Munich, Germany, markets itself as "Museum City" and offers a complete and easily followed guidebook. All of its museums cooperate by helping promote each other, synchronizing their hours, providing maps at each one that include all the locations, etc.

Where is the "Guidebook to Metropolitan Seattle Museums" that this area should have? We are not aware of one, if it exists. The Seattle/King County Convention & Visitors Bureau's annual "Visitors Guide" lists museums but provides little detail. The privately published "ArtGuide Northwest" is attractive and accessible, but it stresses galleries over museums. The Evergreen State Society's "Passport" brochure, lists some of the museums in this region— but not all, since it is a membership organization.

The sooner the metropolitan Seattle area can be "wired" with fiber optics, the better.

Moreover, it also includes many other organizations, foundations, commissions and groups that would be of little interest to most visitors.

The Seattle Art Museum, which opened in a new Robert Venturi-designed building in late 1991, has Asian, Northwest Indian and African art collections that are among the best in the world. It also retains a fine museum of Far Eastern art at its former site in Seattle's Volunteer Park. The Pilchuck School, a workshop for glass artists near Arlington, north of Everett, is a unique institution that draws students and teachers from many different countries. It has clearly established this area (as a February 1992 *Smithsonian* magazine article noted) as one of the world centers in glass art. And several smaller museums in the area—the Burke and Henry museums on the University of Washington Campus, the Frye Art Museum, and the Bellevue and Tacoma Art Museums, often exhibit the work of international artists. The Museum of Flight, which opened in July 1987 at Boeing Field just south of downtown Seattle, has a remarkable collection of aircraft that is rivaled in this country only by the Smithsonian's Air and Space Museum in Washington, D.C. It is gradually gaining an international reputation.

A number of new museums have been proposed that could meet standards of international significance. The $12 million Odyssey Contemporary Maritime Museum is planned at Pier 66, former Port of Seattle headquarters, as part of the Central Waterfront Revitalization Project. Scheduled to open in 1995, the new museum will focus on international trade, oceanography, fisheries and other maritime topics. A $3-million, 13,000-square-foot Museum of Doll Art recently opened in Bellevue, to display the world-class, 2,000-doll collection of Rosalie Whyel. The East King County Convention and Visitor Bureau expects the doll museum to become a major attraction, thanks in part to its location near Bellevue's new convention center. Also, a new Jimi Hendrix Museum of rock-'n-roll has been proposed by Microsoft co-founder Paul Allen to commemorate the life of the rock guitarist who attended Garfield High School; it has the potential to become a showcase for the internationally acclaimed Seattle rock-music scene, including "grunge" and "rap." The Seattle City Council, in a unanimous vote, authorized Seattle Center officials to negotiate a long-term agreement with backers of the museum, which would be financed solely with private donations.

Joint marketing and promotion of our museums would greatly enhance each one individually and the region collectively. Our area, without even straining, can distinguish itself much more by the thoughtful promotion of its museum collections.

Telecommunications

29. RECOMMENDATION: Metropolitan Seattle should build on its existing corporate and technological resources to make this region a world-leading telecommunications center. All major institutions, including government agencies, schools, colleges and universities, libraries, and hospitals—as well as homes and offices—should be linked with fiber-optic cable and integrated wireless networks. Let the private sector compete for this business rather than attempting a government-operated program.

There is no single step that could put metropolitan Seattle on the cutting edge of world telecommunications faster than connecting the entire region with fiber optic and wireless networks. Fiber-optic technology can enormously increase access to the vast quantities of information now available electronically. This step would eliminate the electronic bottleneck that now prevents passage of huge amounts of information over traditional copper telephone wires or coaxial TV cable. No American city has done this comprehensively, but the first one that does will immediately establish itself as a world leader and become a focus of international attention. Consider Hong Kong, which has laid fiber-optic cables across most of its territory; Singapore, which has undertaken a campaign to become a completely wired "technopolis," and Amsterdam, which hopes to become a telecommunications port linking Europe with the world.

Seattle, meanwhile, is ideally prepared for leadership in this field, given the strength of corporate and individual expertise resident here. This strength is found in telephone and wireless companies, both. Fiber is the transport medium for modern communications, as telecommunications analyst (and Discovery Institute Senior Fellow) George Gilder says, and wireless is the access means of the future.

In addition, such a step could help to alleviate the region's transportation congestion problems, as more people could work from their homes. In Atlanta, for instance, the Telecommute Atlanta Project (TAP) has been organized by 60 major businesses, with a goal of making that city the telecommuting capital of the U.S. At Discovery Institute's May 1993 conference, Craig McCaw of McCaw Cellular Communications Inc. called on the region to create a new vision of community, in which new electronic communications technologies—including teleconferencing and personal communication devices—dominated the traditional automobile culture.

On the U.S. national level, funding is available through a federal program, the National Resource Education Network, which is part of the High Performance Computing Initiative passed by Congress. Also, the federal Cable Television Act of 1992 approved new regulations to allow all regional telephone companies to transmit video programs over their lines, thus competing head-to-head with cable TV companies. The action is expected to encourage the phone companies to speed up installation of fiber-optic lines.

Actually, both GTE and US WEST, which provide telephone service to most of the Seattle metropolitan area, have a great deal of fiber optic cable already in place, and are installing more rapidly. GTE is building "smart parks" where fiber is laid before office buildings are constructed, and the company is running "fiber to the curb" at a new housing development north of Seattle. US WEST

> *The merger of McCaw with AT&T will no doubt open the door to even more innovative telecommunications projects.*

announced in February 1993 that it would begin testing a fiber-optic network to provide 100,000 customers with a wide range of video, voice and data services by the end of 1994. The company hopes to hook up 500,000 more customers in 1995. And TCI Cablevision in March 1993 announced that it would begin installing $40 million worth of new fiber-optic cable over the next two years to serve its 170,000 Seattle-area customers. Other cable-TV companies are making similar plans. The spread of fiber networks could and should be spurred by promising new applications such as telecommuting, transportation management, home schooling and interactive health-care systems, which are all likely to boom in the next few years (and, not incidentally, help relieve traffic congestion as well.)

The City of Seattle, which in 1992 imposed a temporary moratorium on new fiber-optic attachments to utility poles, has floated the idea of creating a new city utility to run such communications systems. That would be a mistake; the government should let the private sector take the lead. Nobody can know how the new and constantly changing telecommunications technologies will play out (and certainly no government office can know), so competition is essential to determine what is best and cheapest. These technologies are not static assets like roadways (despite the frequent analogy) or electric power facilities. If the city tries to usurp the field by law, the taxpayers are likely to get saddled with a rapidly obsolescent system—a high-tech white elephant— and they also will have dealt a blow to private competition and creativity. Instead, metropolitan governments should encourage the competitive private sector to move ahead as quickly as possible, because the sooner the area can be wired with fiber optics, the better.

Few other cities have made much progress either, although Electric Lightwave operates a fiber-optic network in Portland. GTE's experimental fiber-optic network in Cerritos, Calif., is another potential model, although relatively limited in size. Already private companies are realizing fiber optics' potential: For example, the Seattle-based construction firm, Wright-Schuchart, has accessed fiber-optic lines to connect with offices in Hawaii and Guam, which it estimates save the company $200,000 a year in telecommunications costs.

In addition, the region should strongly encourage US WEST and GTE to continue digitalizing all their telephone equipment to increase capacity through Integrated Services Digital Networks (ISDN), which can use existing copper telephone cables to transmit voice, text, images and video at high speeds. Again, the technology is already available, and costs are dropping rapidly. These systems are an excellent way to provide a bridge between existing technology and the fiber-optic and wireless networks that will be more efficient, but will take longer to develop.

Last, but not least, recognizing the complementary nature of fiber and wireless technologies, cellular systems should be encouraged, too. The donation of $1 million by Craig McCaw, chairman and CEO of McCaw Communications, Inc., to the Seattle Commons project, with the hope of eventually building a wireless cellular communications network for all offices and homes in the neighborhood, would be a marvelous demonstration project and attract worldwide attention. The merger of McCaw with AT&T, announced in August 1993, will no doubt open the door to even more innovative regional and national telecommunications projects.

Zoos

30. RECOMMENDATION: Metropolitan Seattle should give more support to the international activities of its zoos, especially the new regional/international Center for Wildlife Conservation, which will focus on Native Northwest and Pacific Rim endangered and threatened species.

Seattle's Woodland Park Zoological Gardens is probably more widely recognized for excellence nationally and internationally than locally. It has received the highest rating for zoos from the Humane Society of the United States and the American Association of Zoological Parks and Aquariums. It has been ranked among the best in the country by *The Washington Post, USA Today* and *Parade Magazine.* It has become world-renowned for its model natural habitats, such as the gorilla exhibit, African savanna and Asian tropical forest, which have been widely imitated. It has established exchange programs with zoos in several of Seattle's Sister Cities, including Kobe, Japan; Chongqing, China; Surabaya, Indonesia; and Christchurch, New Zealand. Tacoma's Point Defiance Zoo and the Seattle Aquarium emphasize international exhibits as well.

And a new group still in its infancy, the Center for Wildlife Conservation, is focusing on preservation of endangered and threatened species from the Pacific Northwest and the Pacific Rim, with the goal of creating model preserves and breeding centers in other nations. The idea originated at Woodland Park Zoo, which provided initial impetus and funding. It is co-sponsored by Point Defiance Zoo, the Seattle Aquarium, Northwest Trek and the University of Washington's Institute for Environmental Studies. "We've created a regional network, which is positive in and of itself," said Bob Davidson, executive director of the Woodland Park Zoological Society. The Center won a $300,000 grant from the U.S. Fish & Wildlife Service to begin operations, and will seek private donations as well. It is modeled after similar organizations at the Bronx Zoo and the San Diego Zoo, which have programs in Africa and the Americas.

Woodland Park Zoo has an active program of exchanging staff with other zoos around the world, which helps develop expertise and an attitude of stewardship toward wildlife. In all, about 20 Woodland Park zookeepers have gone overseas, while a dozen foreign zookeepers have come here. This effort should be continued and expanded. In addition, the zoo has exchanged animals with several foreign zoos.

These programs all deserve more recognition and support, because animals have a universal appeal to people from almost all nations. Zoos can be an excellent forum for educating people in principles of wildlife conservation and habitat protection, which have become truly global issues.

Part III

*Discussion
and
Debate*

Discovery Institute invited an array of leaders, scholars, and experts—from the Pacific Northwest and beyond—to examine a draft version of its International Seattle report. Their thoughts and ideas, presented at public conference on May 6, 1993 in Seattle, helped shape the final version of the report. Their perspectives, some of which are excerpted here, offer important insights on the practical challenges facing metropolitan Seattle as it seeks to become more globally competitive. —John Hamer and Bruce Chapman

1. Why Does Metropolitan Seattle Need an International Strategy, and What Should It Include?

"The United States' great urban regions had better start hustling if they expect to compete with their competitors...."

NEAL R. PEIRCE, **Syndicated Columnist and author** of *Citistates: How Urban America Can Prosper in a Competitive World.*

Virtually every monopoly in today's international economy, whether it's in services or in manufacturing, is crumbling. Enterprises find themselves threatened by competitors ready to spring up quite suddenly on any continent. Markets mature and peak and wither with amazing speed. Nothing is proprietary. An item like an IBM PC quickly becomes almost like another commodity, ready to be duplicated and cloned across the globe. In the past, an industry might be able to get along with internal inefficiencies and a mediocre workforce and a lot of local pollution and weak local transportation links.

But no longer. Today's industries don't enjoy that protective envelope of time and space. They must, among other things, exercise some pretty rigorous control over their costs and they need access to vital resources, human and physical. They must be able to hire a competent workforce. They need to be able to move people and goods cost-effectively. They need basic water and sanitation needs fulfilled. They need clean air. They need an environment not plagued by crime. They have major concerns about quality of life for their employees.

Not a single one of those needs can be supplied fully by the single municipality in which the industry is located. All of them are first and foremost metropolitan-wide regional issues. It's this regional focus that must drive us to visualize our great urban and suburban areas as "citistates." Imagine a visitor from another planet approaching the dark side of Earth in our time. He or she would quickly note the clusters of light where humans congregate in great numbers. Approaching any one of them, he would see a fully integrated organism, a concentration of human development of roads and rivers and bridges and buildings, people and vehicles, air, water, energy, interacting closing together. This is clearly the late 20th and the 21st Century "citistate"—the closely intertwined, interrelated geographic, economic, environmental entity that describes our civilization today.

Demographics underscore its reality. As world population rushes into metro regions with hurricane velocity, these areas are where the people are. In this nation in 1950, we had 14 metro areas with over a million people. In the last Census, we had 39 such regions, and they represented for the first time a majority of this country.

Citistates resonate through history. Before there were nation states, there were citistates. You can trace them back to antiquity, to Athens and Sparta and Syracuse. Measured by historic time, nation states are relative newcomers, having arisen to conduct great campaigns of transoceanic colonization and to launch great land wars across the face of Europe. Of course, we will continue to need nation states for such roles as social support systems, income transfer for the poor, air safety, and global military police actions.

But what natural law says that nation states' absolute dominance must remain for all time?

We now see a remarkable confluence of events taking place. Telecommunications have advanced so rapidly that messages and data and money transfers generated in our citistate financial centers now leap

national boundaries in nanoseconds, with no permission granted by the nation state. Investment capital, the mother's milk of urban economic development, becomes increasingly mobile. Trade barriers are crumbling, opening distant markets—and

---

In the past, an industry might be able to get along with internal inefficiencies and a mediocre workforce and a lot of local pollution and weak local transportation links. But no longer.

---

making it much more difficult, as the Europeans are discovering, to subsidize and sustain politically favored regions. And nation states are losing a real measure of their sovereignty: control over their currencies. The walls against immigration are falling down; we can't control who lives within the country. Free trade agreements are proliferating. And the one activity nation states were best at, the use of brute force, amassing huge armies and preparing for war, subsides with the end of the Cold War.

These are the reasons why the United States' great urban regions had better start hustling if they expect to compete effectively with their competitors spread from Seoul to Singapore and Oslo to Osaka and Berlin to Barcelona.

But how does one define the issue of international competitiveness? How broad a slate do you write on?

One approach would be quite narrow, to focus simply on trade relationships, ports and airports, maybe foreign consulates, but not much more. That's in line with quite traditional economic development thinking. The second approach would be to broaden the focus quite significantly to all of the factors that have a pretty indisputable direct linkage to how a citistate positions itself internationally.

Discovery Institute's "International Seattle" report represents a really exciting breakthrough. It's the most thoughtful review I've seen in any region on the multiple and fascinating ways that a citistate starts the conscious process of thinking internationally. The report covers, in very provocative detail, obvious issues of airports, trade, tourism, cruise ships, international conferences, consulates, trade offices, sister cities, and telecommunications. But then the report goes on to a number of less obvious but truly vital issues for international positioning. I was especially impressed by the case for enlarging the geographic scope and mission of the Trade Development Alliance of Greater Seattle to all of the four counties of your region, and from trade to the overall strategy for a globally competitive economy.

The report has valuable recommendations on Cascadia and the special Seattle-Vancouver tie. I admire the quality of life section, including critical questions on urban livability, shaping growth without stifling regulation, infill development and landscaping, and the role of the "Mountains to the Sound Greenway." Regional rapid-rail transit and the potential of a fast train link to Vancouver get the consideration they deserve. The variety of ideas for enriching the international curriculum and outreach of the University of Washington showed careful homework and imaginative direction. I was pleased to see the focus on enhancing the language skill of your regional population.

It's a truly superb report and will soon, if not immediately, set the standard for other regions coast to coast as they look to their international futures. However, a serious look at today's citistate and its international positioning can carry one to a third and even broader level of debate and analysis. The land-use issue, for example, switches from local zoning disputes to a question of the physical shape of a region, how decisions are made about where people work, live and recreate, and the environmental consequences. The image of city centers, their appearance and vitality, becomes not just a challenge for downtown leaders, but a question of the entire citistate's image—to itself but even more critically as

a mirror to the world. Economic development becomes a question of whether the region's special capacities have been identified and are being nurtured. Government efficiency becomes an international competitiveness issue, whether vital regional transportation and environmental and human resource needs are being taken care of. Social issues, when you use the broad citistate lens, become a question of the regional society's whole strength and its capacity to see people who are today in trouble

---

Discovery Institute's "International Seattle" report represents a really exciting breakthrough.

---

not just as a social burden but as potentially valuable human resources waiting to become real regional assets. Philanthropy becomes a question of mobilizing untapped resources and helping strategic planning across multiple jurisdictions. School and university issues suddenly have to be viewed in the context of regional workforce preparedness in an era in which brains, not brawn, will be the ticket to economic success. The leadership question takes on demanding new aspects, including the need to supplement political leadership with strong business and citizen and nonprofit group efforts.

The understanding must be common that everyone's goose will be cooked if the citistate fails to face its challenges and starts to slip economically and socially. The stakes are really immense. The challenge is nothing less than transforming American citistates into the far more conscious, cohesive and resilient entities that they must be if we hope to sustain our standard of living, to save ourselves from severe social discord, to maintain our quality of life and enable our communities to cut the economic mustard in a much smaller, more competitive, more intimately interconnected world than any of us ever expected to see.

"It is difficult to comprehend how any city can be a global actor…without a strategy."

PANAYOTIS SOLDATOS, Director, Institute for the Study of International Cities, Montreal.

There is no reason for Seattle not to be international. You are exporting and importing. You have international or foreign organizations. You are hosting international activities. You have a lot of chambers of commerce, linking the U.S. with a number of other international nation states. Many important cities don't have an international airport; you are fortunate to have a good one. Finally, you have an international population, which will bring the cosmopolitan aspect, and allow easier links with the countries of origin of those ethnic groups.

But it is difficult to comprehend how any city can be a global actor, as a state or a multinational firm is a global actor, without a strategy. I have three suggestions on an international strategy for metropolitan Seattle:

❑ First, you have to work on your competitive elements, noted above, to make sure they are developed enough to help you internationally.

❑ Second, you have to make choices. The most difficult thing is that international cities sometimes try to do everything. They try to be strong in every area. It's important for cities which are not London, Tokyo and New York to make choices. Those sometimes are hard choices because they have political, social and economic costs. But you cannot be a general international city performing well in every area. You have to decide where you have comparative advantages and where you can build competitive advantages.

❑ Third, you have to see your city as part of a number of geographic areas. Seattle is in the western part of North America, interacting with British Columbia and other areas of the Canadian West. Then you have to see Seattle in the Pacific Rim area; how can you best position yourself there? And you have to see Seattle in the more global arena. You need different strategies for different areas of deployment. All are not the same. You have to seek trade within a number of environments.

Take the gateway approach. Everybody likes to be a gateway, and you are in an area where many cities are gateways. You can be a gateway, competing with other gateways. It's not just urban marketing, to go out and say we are a gateway for the Pacific. Others are saying the same thing. You have to see what makes a gateway city, what it takes in terms of policies and strategies.

2. Can Metropolitan Seattle Really Succeed in the World League?

"Can Boeing be world-class if it has to live and operate in less than a world-class environment?"

DOUGLAS P. BEIGHLE, Senior Vice President, The Boeing Company.

My comments are from two perspectives. First, from a Boeing perspective, and second, from someone who's lived in Seattle for 33 years and has lived downtown for 12. I've seen a lot of change in the city, and a lot of change in Boeing. Right now at Boeing we're changing to stay ahead. A number of us have gone to Japan on study missions. We're sending all of our employees through a course in world-class competitiveness. We're implementing a Total Quality Management system, because we know to survive we've got to have world-class employees and a world-class environment in which to work. Our suppliers have to qualify in a very rigorous quality system, D1-9000. Why? Because we can't be world-class at Boeing and have second-class suppliers. But can Boeing be world-class if it has to live and operate in less than a world-class environment? Can it successfully change to stay ahead if it is not supported by an infrastructure that also changes to stay ahead?

Let's look at Seattle. We've got a lot going for us on a positive side: a significant export base, great natural beauty and setting, and hospitable people. We're ahead in many areas. But what are the negatives? Seattle, almost by default, has become an international city. To stay an international city today you can't be static, you've got to be dynamic. Is Seattle dynamic? Is this region dynamic? Puget Sound basically has a no-growth attitude. Growth generally is regarded as a burden, not a benefit.

We've expressed these concerns, starting with a speech Boeing Chairman Frank Shrontz gave a couple of years ago to the Chamber of Commerce. They are concerns that I expressed on the Governor's Economic Development and Environmental Enhancement Task Force prior to the start of this legislative session. We communicated our frustration with regulations and bureaucrats. For almost two months this year, I drove by an open ditch along Marginal Way on my way to the office. We just finished our new cafeteria, but we couldn't put the curb back in and had about a one-foot ditch on the edge of the road—with warning signs so someone wouldn't drive into it—because of some bureaucratic squabble on getting a building inspector out to look at it so we could pour the concrete. And this went on for almost two months. We've seen non-value-added delays in trying to get plant licenses that range from 18 months at Everett to 28 months down the Duwamish Corridor. We're still hung up at Longacres. Our Systems Integration Lab, which is critical for the 777 program, is out near our headquarters. We're going to replicate the 777 systems and get the expe-

rience in the lab for that airplane so it's completely service-ready when we deliver it. We thought we had the building permit program well outlined. Then suddenly we found out that because of power usage we had to get an extra permit from Seattle City Light. And right in the middle of a critical timepath, the person who was handling the permit

Douglas P. Beighle

Puget Sound basically has a no-growth attitude.

went on vacation, and locked the thing in his drawer for three weeks. It cost us a million dollars in delays. I can go on and on and on. The problem is, there's an attitude of "growth is a burden," and if we can stall it and delay it, it won't happen.

Yes, there are some encouraging examples. I heard Governor Lowry, right after he took office, state to the Economic Development conference that he was going to do everything possible to see that Boeing's next airplane was built in this area. We've seen the City of Tukwila step up to a master plan on the Duwamish Corridor and we expect that we will be able to get building permits in a very reasonable time period in the future. We saw the Pierce County Commissioners, because they felt that our plant at Frederickson would be a desirable neighbor, set up a team of all the County department heads to work the problems, and we were able to get our building permits.

But, the overall trend is anti-business. Prior to the '93 Legislature, we had a tax structure that discouraged start-up businesses because the B&O tax was on revenues, not on income. Taxes were a burden. You see numbers that we're anywhere from the 14th-highest burdened state to much higher. Basically, there's a no-growth attitude and little or no investment in tourism, even though it's one of our strongest economic areas. And then came the

We've got a lot going for us…[but] to stay an international city you can't be static.

93rd legislative session. The April 30 *Puget Sound Business Journal,* in describing this session, quoted one lobbyist that this was "the session from hell." It quoted another one: "This is the worst session overall for small and large business in 25 years."

It was recently announced that a Seattle startup firm associated with the Fred Hutchinson Cancer Center had decided to build its factory in Rhode Island, creating two hundred jobs. Why? Because of incentives from Rhode Island to build that factory. We told the Economic Development Task Force for the Governor that this area is not competitive. We suggested a benchmarking study to compare this area with other areas, because we've seen what other areas would do to attract new facilities. Anytime Boeing even makes noise that we're interested in building something, the offers roll in. And what happens in Seattle? We get delayed for 18 months and pay $50 million in fees to build a facility up at Everett.

Even if the regulatory environment is more costly, you can live with that if you can get some certainty. But when it doesn't bring you certainty so you can't operate on a reliable timetable, that's a really serious problem for business. Where you're planning ahead, where you've got a definitive endline you're working

against, you've got to know how you're going to come out in the process.

So, when you read through the list of what is a world-class city, does this area really stack up? We don't have destination resorts, which B.C. and Oregon both do. I ask you to judge yourself whether our two daily newspapers are world-class. We do have a very fine public television station in KCTS-9, which covers two countries, both British Columbia and Western Washington.

Concerning transportation, I think without a doubt we've probably got the most disreputable fleet of taxis in the world. I think most high-school students would be trading down if they traded their cars for a taxi here. I don't know why we can't regulate our taxicabs like other countries do, and require that they be modern and don't have the fenders all banged off, and have seatbelts that work. As for congestion, Seattle has more automobiles registered inside the city limits than we have residents. The draft Seattle Master Plan that was just released predicts that our traffic congestion will increase ten-fold if we don't get our problems solved with our freeways. Doing nothing is simply not acceptable in the transportation side. We've got to finish our HOV lanes. We need better bus service. People say, "Well, people won't ride the buses." But at our Everett facility, in relocation of the 777 program, we made a real effort to get people out of their automobiles and into carpools, vans and buses. Now over 35% of the people at Everett are in one of those three modes of transportation and out of the single-passenger car. And that exceeds the target we had set for ourselves by the end of the century.

Another thing that a world-class area must have is safety. There's a perception that street crime is a serious problem in downtown Seattle. I live downtown and I walk all over, and I don't particularly worry about it. But people who live in the suburbs tell me they're afraid to come to downtown Seattle at night.

At Sea-Tac Airport, congestion is causing delays in bad weather because we don't have the third runway. We need more capacity by the turn of the century or we're going to have serious problems. One plus is that with Mick Dinsmore (Chief Executive Officer, Port of Seattle), the airport and the port are reaching out and they're now much more customer-first oriented. Boeing probably has anywhere from a hundred to a thousand people a week come through SeaTac—air crews coming in for training, customers, etc. Before, our drivers would be hassled when they went out to pick them up. We'd have our vans towed away. Now, we've got cooperation. They're helping us with VIPs coming through international customs. Before, we were ignored, and I would really like to compliment Mick and what he's doing to help turn that attitude around.

Finally, I would like to talk about education and a world-class workforce. There's nothing more important to a world-class business than a world-class workforce. And we are putting a lot of our energy today into education. Almost half of Boeing's $26 million contribution budget is directed to education, plus more than half of our $5.5 million in-kind budget. Our members are active in education-reform activities nationally and locally. We know that Boeing again someday will be hiring, and we need a supply of employees that are trainable, educated in math, can read and write, and can help us change to stay ahead.

"Our world-class institutions and private sector have done well, but they sort of happened to us."

PAUL SCHELL, Commissioner, Port of Seattle, and Co-Chairman, Discovery Institute.

The metropolitan Seattle region is world-class in many ways. We have a world-class port. We have many world-class private and some semi-public enterprises, thanks to Mr. Boeing and Mr. Gates, which happened without a whole lot of public governmental interference. We have our scenery, and a location that gives us a terrific jumping-off point both to Europe and to Asia. We're only 8 hours away from Europe, even closer than Miami is to Europe in terms of air time. So, we really are correctly positioned in terms of taking advantage of both the European and the Asian opportunity. And we have a world-class public market which the public saved. We have cleaned up a lot of our environmental areas, but that was thanks to folks who had the vision and the wisdom and the courage to proceed.

So our world-class institutions and private sector have done well, but they sort of happened to us. Now I think it is a different ballgame. It is a more competitive world. And the problem is, can we deal with this 21st Century opportunity with our 19th Century organizations? We too often try to fit our problems to the organization. We manipulate the task so it fits our solution, rather than trying to organize to the task. We need to think in terms of strategic alliances and partnerships that are organized to respond to the particular challenge.

There's a lot that's good about this region. There's a lot that needs to be done. My highest priority would be our education system, preparing our next generation to deal with very real challenges. We're doing a poor job of that. We need to give that, as a community, our highest priority. We've got lots of social and economic challenges in front of us, and we need to start to build teams and to allow leadership to occur. That requires an understanding among the public and the media to allow partnering, to allow leadership to make mistakes, to allow risks to be taken. While that may not be as newsworthy as controversy, I somehow think we can never consider ourselves a world-class city when, on the day the Port announced the arrival of China Eastern Airlines, a new trade route from Shanghai to Seattle, the headline story was the possibility only that we might buy a $10,000 couch for the front lobby of the Port headquarters, where we deal with the international trading community.

At the Port, we're doing a lot of partnering, with labor, business, and other governments. We have observed the other very competitive metropolitan regions and what they have been doing for some time. Whether it's Stuttgart or Amsterdam or Singapore (which is the same size as Seattle) or Hong Kong or Kobe, you can't come away but impressed by the attention they've given to their educational systems, their transportation infrastructure, their community spirit. There is a shared sense of destiny and vision. While they have their problems and disagreements, there is no mistake that the people in those regions know where they are going. I don't think we do. We're very satisfied with where we are. We have reason to be, but I'm confident that it won't be that way five years or even three years from now. We should not label every idea or every person who thinks ahead as a "visionary" somehow consigned to an institution, but rather say, "We're going to start to applaud those people, those governments, those organizations that are starting to work together and are trying to think ahead and are willing to take some risks."

In international tourism, I'm convinced a partnering with Vancouver and the Cascadia notion is the way to celebrate our region with some panache. Our local metropolitan transportation system is one we have to deal with in a three-county area. Our educational system may be one we deal with in each county. But let's be unafraid to take a new look at all the ways we get organized and the way our institutions work. The most important asset we have in this community is that we still feel very much in charge, empowered perhaps by early campaigns on freeways and markets and neighborhoods, and by the many caring citizens here. We haven't lost that sense of who's in charge. We're not so quick to blame "them" or the "other guy." If we can build on that sort of spirit, it's our greatest asset.

"Seattle's ability to play in the world league depends on you and me."

HELEN MARIESKIND, President, Sime Health Limited.

Provoked by Discovery's International Seattle report, I've been asking people, "What cities in the world do you think are international?" They always name the usual—Paris, Rome, Hong Kong, Buenos Aires, New York—but not Seattle. So then I ask, "Well, what about Seattle?" And the answer has always been a hesitant, "Yes, well, I guess so. We have a port, an Asian population, Boeing, trade, tourists come here." But there's always a hesitancy, a somewhat reluctant admission. Perhaps this reluctance is just part of our seemingly eternal Northwest politeness, our unwillingness to be passionate that possibly an infusion of enough coffee will help to jazz up.

But like everything else in life, we must first believe it ourselves. If we want to play in the world league, we need to get an attitude that we can and we are. And I don't think this attitude is one of false pride. Expanding on just a few points:

First, the people. I love looking at cities when I travel around the world from the perspective of what I call the "facescape"—what the people who are walking around look like. And the facescape of Seattle is really interesting and has become increas-

ingly varied and international over the 16 years I've lived here. One of the reasons Sime-Darby is happy to be here is that my Asian colleagues feel comfortable here. There are people who look just like them when they walk around the street. And the range of languages one hears has also expanded. But in the interests of maturing and thinking as a world-league player, I'd like to make a pitch for dropping the emphasis on "foreign" when we talk about other languages. They are simply other languages which people of different ethnicities speak. The more we accept that notion, the less scary other languages become to learn and to integrate into our everyday usage.

For Sime Health, both as part of a Malaysia-based conglomerate and as an international business based in metropolitan Seattle, this area works well. From a business perspective, Seattle works for us as a global player for seven principal reasons:

❑ There are good import and transportation facilities thanks to the Port and experienced custom brokerages. But I do want to echo the sentiments expressed earlier: we must manage the Seattle-Tacoma port competition. I appreciate a good sales pitch. But as a customer, it takes my time and energy and distracts me from business to be pitched.

❏ Seattle has excellent communications systems, and an advantageous location. With our office open from 6:00 a.m. to 6:00 p.m., we can have at least six hours contact with any company within our territory, and an hour or two in contact with Malaysia before we go home. Phone and fax links out of Seattle are excellent and we rarely experience difficulty on our side in being able to communicate out or receive incoming messages.

❏ When all is said and done about the romance of international trade—and believe me, there are days it doesn't seem too romantic—companies do it to make money. Seattle, with less than two million people in the metropolitan area, is not a huge market. This could be seen as a drawback for companies here. But when the accessibility Seattle gives to the U.S./Canadian/Mexican markets is considered, the smallness of the immediate market is irrelevant. In fact, the smallness becomes a plus. This is a manageable city. We can run errands, meet people, have multiple meetings on the same day, change plans, get our containers delivered on short notice, get to government offices easily, get things done, and eat well. Visitors can sleep well, our staff can live, breathe and play well in Seattle. Stop for a moment and think of how few cities in the world this can be said. In many cities, one or two appointments per day—at the most—is standard, simply because you can't get about easily. Bangkok and Mexico City are nightmares to do business in.

❏ The workforce here is diverse. Sime-Darby is a multi-ethnic company and I committed Sime Health to reflecting the ethnic diversity of the Americas. In Seattle, we can have a workforce that meets this goal. Sime Health has several different nationalities on its staff and we can do business in 15 languages, including many Asian languages.

❏ Services are a fifth reason. I'm including education as a service, although it can easily be considered under workforce. But education is not just getting workers who can spell and count, although that is a really good beginning. Metropolitan Seattle has an educated population from which to draw. But before we sit back and congratulate ourselves,

let me tell you as an employer reviewing applicants that there's a great deal of room for growth. But there are the resources here to train people—good universities, excellent libraries, vocational and technical educational institutions and night classes. And there are, of course, excellent law and accounting firms, ad agencies, printers, etc.

Paul Schell, Helen Marieskind

For Sime Health, the metropolitan Seattle area works well.

But I want to interject a caution here against complacency. We, along with other companies, are being actively courted by other cities —most notably Atlanta and Miami. Atlanta is particularly an effective campaigner, with a marvelous "Sell Georgia" room at Georgia Power. You can sit in this room at a crystallite table and push a button and have anyplace in Georgia flash on the table with an accompanying screen to show everything about its demographics, finances, opportunities, etc., instantly. I suggest we duplicate such a thing in Seattle. I'm not of a mind to move to Atlanta, I simply note that there are cities with very proactive selling programs and there could be some lessons here for Seattle. And a side note: I am involved with CARE, the international relief organization which recently announced that it was relocating its offices from New York to Atlanta. I think the recommendation in Discovery Institute's report for attracting a large international volunteer quasi-governmental agency is terrific. If Atlanta can do it, why not Seattle?

❏ Sixth, consider financial resources. Seattle

banks can lend money and there are several able to serve a growing company. But we do need much better banking services for international business. Bankers, please, just get to know the banks down in the Americas, know the system, so you can advise a new business on which banks you can even trust.

❑ The seventh reason is ambience, and we're back to the facescape again. Business can be done anywhere there's an item to sell and two people, at least one of whom has some money. Business can be done in Seattle in an ambience that is compatible with many cultures. We make a great mistake if we underestimate the importance of feeling comfortable. Everyone likes to be among their own kind. For those of us who travel a lot to foreign places, yes, it's exotic, it's exciting and educational and all the rest, but there often comes a time when you just say, "I want my own food, to talk my own language and to easily understand the humor and the nuances."

Seattle has the capability to provide that diversity and that comfort. And people like to have fun, too, in their own way. Seattle, ladies and gentlemen, needs a classy night life.

Beyond believing in ourselves, we must practice internationalism. This goes way beyond inviting a foreigner to make it a more interesting dinner party or hosting a tourist or exchange student. As parents, we must commit our childrearing to internationalism. Teach tolerance, practice diversity, show our children there are other ways to live, to do things, to believe, to see the world. Governments can only do so much and so can business, but the bottom line is that governments and businesses are made up of people with families. They're made up of all of us here. We must look to ourselves and make our own personal commitment. At the end of the day, Seattle's ability to play in the world league depends on you and me.

"We are a global company and the software industry, in particular, is a global industry."

KIMBERLY ELLWANGER, **Corporate Attorney, Government Affairs, Microsoft Corporation.**

In order to give you a sense of Microsoft's perspective on these issues, it would be helpful to tell you a little bit about the company. We get a lot of press, but we're only 17 years old and many people don't understand really what it is that we do. We develop, market and support a wide range of systems and applications software for personal computers. As a company whose products are intellectual in nature, people are our most important asset. Thus, it's essential that we nurture an atmosphere in which creative thinking thrives and employees are able to develop to their fullest potential. Another important fact about the company is that over 55% of our revenues come from export sales. We develop products in 25 languages, we have 39 subsidiaries and we market our products in over 200 countries.

One of the trade associations that we belong to, Business Software Alliance, commissioned a report earlier this spring that was prepared by Economists, Inc. The report looked at the impact of the software industry on the domestic and the global economy. I want to note a couple of highlights from the report.

The computer software industry is the

Math and science education is critical for our company to continue to thrive in this region... To create more jobs, we must have a good educational structure.

fastest-growing major industry in the United States. Its increases in economic contributions of over 269%

over the past ten years compare with a growth of about 34% generally. The prepackaged sector of the software industry holds an estimated 75% of the worldwide market share. The reason for citing those statistics is that we are a global company and the software industry, in particular, is a global industry.

Well, why are we located here? To be quite candid, it's because Bill Gates' parents live here. Maybe the more relevant question is, "What is it about this region that can attract high-technology companies to locate here?" Because people are our biggest asset, it's essential to our company and the high-technology sector in general to be able to recruit and retain quality employees. It is important to create an educational and scientific milieu that is going to attract those kinds of people to this area. Math and science education is critical for our company to continue to thrive in this region. And not just for our company, but to create startup companies, to create more jobs, we must have a good educational structure.

The University of Washington is a great institution, but a lot of people are surprised to learn that the institution from which Microsoft hires most of its employees is the University of Waterloo, located in Canada. There is something about their teaching programs that enables them to turn out students who think creatively in math and science. We also hire a lot of people from the University of Washington and are working with them to continue their excellence and their leadership. But for the industries of the future, it is essentially critical to be able to teach that kind of creative thinking.

Microsoft's director of international marketing recently was asked, "How is Seattle as an international city?" And he said, "Well, it's a good city. We like doing business here. It's a friendly city. But if I had one criticism it's the lack of direct flights from Seattle to other major cities around the world." There are many employees at Microsoft who do a lot of traveling. It's nice to be able to get places directly rather than have to spend a lot of time in airports. And so, we were pleased that the Puget Sound Regional Council has adopted a recommendation to deal with the airport capacity problem.

"Negatives can become positives, and in fact can be the source of energy and dynamic competition…"

JIM STREET, Seattle City Council, and past President, Puget Sound Regional Council.

The Puget Sound Regional Council is right in the middle of the development of a regional economic strategy. The impetus for that effort came out of the trip that occurred a year ago to Europe, organized by the Greater Seattle Chamber of Commerce and Seattle and other entities in the region. Out of that trip came a commitment for a private-public partnership to really sit down and develop, as a multi-county region, a vision and a strategy and action plan about where we're going, not next year but in the next 20 years in terms of our position in the world economy. This Discovery Institute report offers a tremendous input to the regional economic strategy. I noticed that it's copyrighted, but we'll have to discuss whether or not at least some of the vision, and certainly a lot of the ideas, will find their way into the regional economic strategy.

If you look at the Port of Seattle, and you consider the lack of critical mass of the Northwest compared to other markets within the United States, that's one of the weaknesses that the Port of Seattle has made a strength in terms of its strategy on containerization, efficiency, and movement of products throughout the United States. I would wager that the Port of Seattle would not be as dynamic and competitive a port as it is today if it had been nestled in some comfortable large market where the need to compete nationally was not an urgent factor. Look at Japan. If there was ever a place that lacked land resources, had all kinds of negatives, and has turned them into positives, it's a tremendous example. So negatives can become positives, and in fact can be the source of energy and dynamic competition, finding niches that make a region truly competitive.

3. What is the Role of New Communications Technologies in Creating the Metropolitan Seattle of the Future?

"We have our wireless seeds, as it were, of change."

CRAIG McCAW, Chairman and Chief Executive Officer, McCaw Cellular Communications.

Man's record is not particulary good with respect to our cities. As you probably recall, human beings first settled down when they discovered seeds and there was a reason to stay in one place. Otherwise, we are probably realistically nomadic by nature. In creating cities every time it was done historically, cataclysmic events destroyed those cities. Most of those events were disease-related, related to bringing people together in very close proximity.

The fundamental purpose of the city began with security or economics; certainly social benefits were also high on the list. Cities were later put together as part of the Industrial Revolution, essentially making it very efficient for people to be together. But in all cases you've seen cities go through a growth and a fall. And there is probably no city in the world that has not had the fall unless it is a young city like Seattle.

The Industrial Revolution had an idea about the value of people that was very different from the one that we stand for today. Telecommunications, the computer and, of course, the airplane have changed the way we view people. But fundamentally, people are not tools because machines can do more efficiently what we can and do it much better with higher quality.

What people are used for is creativity. The cities therefore must recognize the changed environment. Mayor Norm Rice has envisioned Seattle's potential "urban villages." But fundamentally, look at Seattle today, and you see a lot of degradation of the quality of life that brought us here in the first place. There's been degradation in the natural environment that makes Seattle attractive and causes it to be a desirable international destination.

We have continued to grow in the style of the Industrial Revolution. That is, you start out with a city, you grow around it and then you build suburbs

> *You don't necessarily have to work from your home, but you should work close to your home and perhaps walk to work.*

because you don't like what you had in the city and you keep running away from those elements. In just a few years 60% of business has moved out of cities in this country.

This longing to move away from what we created causes people every weekend in New York to drive hours to get to Long Island—which is, in itself, fundamentally destroyed by human action. The routes, the transportation links, all of that fail when you do not address making the central core attractive. Essentially, each city has gone through a sequence that is predictable by its nature and you see the seeds of it here in Seattle. The community is suffering serious degradation as a result of air pollution and congestion of the freeways.

It wasn't many years ago that people stayed in town, and all the elements of the environment were there and easy to access. You now see people moving in increasing numbers to places like Sun Valley or rural California, and doing their work from there—people with a personal computer publishing from Friday Harbor. But of course, Friday Harbor on a summer's day now reminds you of Nantucket and the congestion repeats itself. We then flee across the border to Canada and beyond the 50th parallel, where there aren't many people. But how far can you go? And do you want to run away from what's happening to Seattle? Certainly as we grow and as the environment changes, we recognize that further, more thoughtful, change must occur for our community to prosper in the future.

Projects like the Seattle Commons represent a very logical alternative to destroying what we have and then moving on. And while we at McCaw have had a tiny role in it, others have made a vast contribution; and the effort is still in its infancy.

The idea is, if you remember what Seattle was like not many years ago (and it still is very beautiful) you have to recognize the impact you're having and perhaps undo it. There's a lovely lake in Seattle, in fact, a series of lakes. Lake Union is somewhat polluted, but not nearly as polluted as before the efforts of Metro and a lot of others. But a lot needs to be done to have Seattle avoid the degradation of cities like New York, Los Angeles, and San Francisco. Seattle is now perhaps the most successful city remaining on the West Coast, but usually when you are on those lists it's the beginning of the end, because even more people show up, fleeing Los Angeles. Los Angeles was a paradise a few years ago, a place you would want to go, and even now it's not such a bad place, but the loss of physical security, the loss of the environment, makes it very painful.

We have our wireless seeds, as it were, of change. We view that technology above all and perhaps the personal computer as changing the options that a city and a community have in how they organize. We see that very much in the mode where people work closer to where they live, preserving the environment and keeping the greatest luxury of all, which is the ability to walk from one place to an-

other and not be overcome with diesel exhaust fumes. That means reorganizing the way the city lives and works—and now is the time to do it.

We are lucky that we have clean industry and yet we aren't changing the way we organize people. Again, the commuting in Seattle, owing to our natural environment, our lovely water and mountains, and the way they've restricted us will prevent

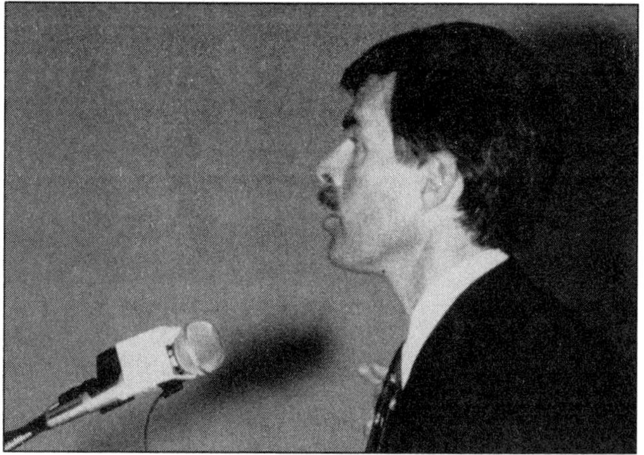

Craig McCaw

us from evolving in an orderly fashion if we don't institute the change we think is necessary. You can't run much further. The mountains and water will see to that.

We propose that you consider for Seattle the idea that stability of the community can be preserved by necessitating far less travel and allowing employees to work closer to where they live. It is only really a matter of our will to do it. The technology is so close now that if we plan today it will be here in time.

Essentially, we as humans are the vital resource, not machines. They are our tools, and we should not be used in a degrading manner. We should be optimized and therefore able to return to our nomadic ways and do more as we please during the day. Americans are the most creative people in the world and through our diversity as a society have the ability to use human mind power as our particular resource. Microsoft has aptly proved that we can make a lot more money with something even less tangible than an airwave, for instance, a piece of software written out of nothing but ideas. Microsoft, as a percentage of revenues, is the most profitable major corporation in America today. So we have in our backyard the most obvious examples of why we need to change. And why the economics should not be business versus the environment and people but should minimize the ill-effects that come from the degradation of the environment.

If you put human beings at the center and give them power through personal-communications devices, the pattern in which people would travel an hour to the office to sit at the end of a six-foot cord and spend their whole day talking to people in other parts of the world doesn't make a lot of sense. And what destroys the city is that travel, that commuting at particular fixed hours, and all the roads and infrastructure. Our idea is that people should travel to be together and not to work, which is a fairly simple concept. With the power of personal computation and wireless communications, you put the people at the center of their own universe and they're productive in and of themselves. Therefore, they regain control of their lives, happiness, and security.

The city is for the social activity. Economic activities can be cared for with proper infrastructure. Therefore, you essentially preserve the ability to have communities of interest. I think we have it at our doorstep. We could be the first city to do it and we're the most logical city to do it. It requires a fundamental change in the way we organize people. Obviously, we at McCaw are a company just like every other: People tend to commute to the office

longer distances. They're running away as well, even though we have the pleasure of operating out of Carillon Point over in Kirkland, which is a terrific place and helps keep our people off the freeway. They even can row to work or take their boats when coming from Seattle. But people who live in Seattle perhaps should work in Seattle. We shouldn't ask people to travel these long distances.

To compete internationally we also need an infrastructure that allows people to work around the clock. If you want to deal with Stuttgart this afternoon and Tokyo later in the day, you must compose a work day that allows you to do that and still enjoy the benefits of a family and the other qualities of life we want to preserve.

This argues for a new infrastructure which gives people flexibility, which doesn't enslave them to particular hours, but again puts them together selectively and creates communities of interest. You don't necessarily have to work from your home but you should work close to your home and perhaps walk to work. And when it's appropriate to be together, you won't have to drive so long on the road because everybody else won't be doing the same thing.

From our perspective at McCaw, we tend to see it very clearly. And all you need is to recognize how close we are to it to know that it's the right solution.

4. What is the City Government's Role in Creating a More International Seattle?

"Our city is working with you... But none of us should think that what we're doing is enough."

MAYOR NORMAN B. RICE, City of Seattle.

I want to compliment John and Bruce for thinking big when it comes to Seattle and its international future. The International Seattle report and its recommendations serve to elevate this issue to a

more urgent plane in our regional consciousness. Some people may agree or disagree with your recommendations, and some might have picked different recommendations as the highest priority today.

But I would hope that nobody would disagree with your central thesis, that Seattle's future depends on its commitment to the international community and that we need to do even more in the years ahead to tap our international potential.

Now, some people might say, "Why worry? We compete in the global market already. We were designated by *Fortune* magazine as the number one city for international business." Well, you'll never hear

Mayor Norman B. Rice

You can quickly lose your competitive edge if you don't watch out.

me saying that. That accolade from Fortune is a good marketing tool, but you can quickly lose your competitive edge if you don't watch out. That's why I took such a strong stand on the airport capacity issue, and that's why my administration worked so hard with the Port to keep American President Lines on our waterfront and to expand their operations. That's why I joined with Mick Dinsmore and Paige Miller on that grueling mission to China to try to land hundreds of new Port jobs, and that's why we're working with the Department of Construction and Land Use to accelerate the permit process even more. International competitiveness is not some God-given right that Seattle will always have. It is something that we must continually be working on and improving.

About a year ago, many local business leaders participated in the European Study Mission sponsored by the City, the Chamber, the Port and the Trade Development Alliance. Likewise, many have

just returned from this year's Chamber inter-city visit. Last year, we went to Europe. This year, we went to Cleveland. I'll let you draw your own conclusions about that. These two study missions both have a lot to teach us.

Last year in Europe, we learned important lessons about education, workforce training and apprenticeship programs. We saw how land-use planning and mass transit could make a region more competitive and more livable at the same time. We saw how they handled trade and tourism promotion in a cooperative way, and the trip highlighted the need for a strong maritime and airport infrastructure as a prerequisite to a healthy international region.

Last week in Cleveland, we saw what happens if there's neglect in your community. We saw what happens if you allow a central city to decay. We saw the lasting scars of a community that was divided over race and economic lines. And we saw the tremendous cost and the decades-long effort that will be required to recover from these problems. Yes, we need to look outward to the possibilities and the needs of an international economy, but we also must look inward to see the fault lines in our own region, to maintain the educational and infrastructure systems that are so vital, to extend the benefits of trade and tourism to every segment of our community.

We just can't clap a bright new coat of paint over the region and say we've got an international city. We've got to make sure that we are looking at the underlying conditions and that we address education, transportation, public safety and community-based economic development, or we're building our international base on a very shaky foundation. And lest you think that this is something that we don't need to worry about, just think about Los Angeles. About ten years ago it was at the top of everybody's list as an international city. But now it isn't even in *Fortune's* top ten.

The "can do" spirit is Seattle, and that's the spirit I think we need to achieve if we're truly going to be an international city. Indeed, that's the kind of spirit we must achieve if we're going to avoid losing the gains that we've already made. We cannot afford to become complacent. Our geographic position alone isn't enough. Anybody who's ever been to Asia knows what I'm talking about. Our competitors are anything but complacent, and if we sit back and if we relax our efforts, and if we fail to create a more cohesive, comprehensive approach to the issues of international competitiveness, then the world is going to pass us by.

All of us can point with pride to what we've accomplished so far. Our region has some of the most successful exporters in history; our ports are among the busiest in the nation; and we have many groups and associations devoted to trade and international relations. And they all do excellent work. Our city is working with you, and we can work together to make sure that we have that foundation we need to look outward. But none of us should think that what we're doing is enough.

I know that some are working to pull together more meetings that will be the next step. I hope they can address what I believe are two critical things: First, all of us have to expand our definition of what constitutes a truly effective international citistate. All the international savvy, and all the trade missions in the world will not keep this region competitive if we allow our environment or our quality of life to suffer. Second, if we're serious about International Seattle, then all of us need to work even harder and learn how to work in greater harmony. The waters are pretty rough out there and the current is strong, but we all need to be pulling together.

5. What Can Metropolitan Seattle Learn from European Cities?

"Our international reputation doesn't come from the city. It comes from our companies."

An Interview via live video conference between Discovery President Bruce Chapman and Manfred Rommel, Mayor of Stuttgart, Germany.

CHAPMAN: Herr Rommel, your city was written up in *The New York Times* recently as the home of the largest floral festival in Europe, is that correct?

ROMMEL: Yes, that's correct. We have a great International Garden Exposition and it looks very nice. We hope to attract a lot of visitors.

CHAPMAN: I wonder if you could tell us how that came about and how you decided to stress that particular aspect of your urban area?

ROMMEL: Stuttgart is the most industrialized city in Western Germany. We have a very concentrated urban structure. In order to bring more quality of life to the city, we decided to have this big Garden Exposition in the center of the city. We were very successful. When the exposition is over, we will have five miles of cultivated parks in the city which make the housing areas around them much more attractive than they used to be. We have a new monorail railway for the exposition, which works without a human driver. We look forward to the future following this exposition with great optimism.

CHAPMAN: Could tell us a little bit about regional cooperation? You're in the Baden Wurttemburg state, and you have a good regional relationship there. Have you been able to cooperate with those communities outside the City of Stuttgart that are still in your general area, and how do you go about doing that?

ROMMEL: We try to cooperate. If we don't ask for money, the cooperation is rather good. But, of course, the suburbs around Stuttgart are not too pleased to do some burden sharing with the City of Stuttgart in the field of public transport and cultural facilities. We are trying to come to an arrangement on this because we think that more and more local activities cannot be successful if they are not being coordinated with our neighbor communities. I hope also to get some support from the state, which will encourage cooperation.

CHAPMAN: What sort of support do you get from your federal government?

ROMMEL: In Germany, the federal government is very much limited to legislation. But we get grants, for instance, for public transport. For investment in transport, we get 60% from the federal government and 25% from the state government. So we could afford a rather expensive system of public transport which is very much needed in this densely populated area in order to make traffic possible. And, of course, we receive also from the federal government of Germany a lot of regulations. The Germans are great producers of regulations. If the Germans see some freedom, they believe it is a gap in the regulation system and fill it out. But in general, we get along rather well also with the federal government.

CHAPMAN: Well, that's not too different from other societies, as a matter of fact. I wonder if you could talk to us a little bit about how your public government, namely, the city, works with the private sector, the entrepreneurial sector of the economy. What cooperation exists there, and how do you go about pursuing it?

ROMMEL: We have a lot of cooperation; we need it. For example, the zoning law in Germany is the responsibility of the cities, and cities are rather independent concerning zoning. Therefore, we have permanent cooperation with the Business Society of Stuttgart. And the Business Society asks for investments to improve the quality of the region, for instance, investment in theaters and cultural facilities. Also investment in water supply and investment against air pollution. We are producing in Stuttgart between 80 and 90 percent of our electricity with nuclear power, which helps keep the air clean. We try also to build streets and roads and to complete our public transport system, which is very expensive. Our Business Society asks for a lot of investment but, of course, the Business Society is less interested in high taxes and leaves it to the

Mayor and to the City Council to solve the problem.

CHAPMAN: Can you tell us, Herr Rommel, what kinds of steps you have taken to create Stuttgart's new reputation as an international community? We know from the trip that Seattle Mayor Norm Rice and others took to Stuttgart last year, that you have achieved a number of important break-

Bruce Chapman, Manfred Rommel

We have a lot of cooperation; we need it.

throughs in the past few years and have established Stuttgart as a prominent international city. How did that happen?

ROMMEL: Stuttgart has been an industrial area for more than a hundred years. But what we did is first to replace the jobs we lost in production by automation, with jobs in services, and we were really successful. Between 1970 and 1987, we lost 70,000 jobs in the city in production, but we replaced them by another 70,000 jobs in services. Of course, our international reputation doesn't come from the city. It comes from our companies. We have really famous automobile and electronics companies. And people in the world know our companies much better than the city itself.

6. Why Should "Cascadia" Be a Foreign Policy Priority for Metropolitan Seattle?

"International policy for a city starts with the nearest border and the nearest foreign city."

JOHN MILLER, former Congressman; Senior Fellow, Discovery Institute; and Chairman of Discovery's Cascadia Corridor Transition Project.

International policy for a city starts with the nearest border and the nearest foreign city. For Seattle, that means the Canadian border, and Vancouver, B.C. It's easy to overlook what's happening in the corridor concentrated along I-5 from B.C. down to Oregon. In a view from a satellite at night 25 miles up, that corridor is an elegant string of lights stretching from Vancouver down to Eugene. Viewed from Customs offices, that corridor is five million vehicular crossings a year in 1985, becoming 11 million in 1992, and 28 million in the year 2000. Viewed by much of the business community, including banks and law firms and even baseball teams, the corridor is becoming one great regional market. But viewed by many citizens, the corridor is an ecotopia that may soon become an environmental nightmare.

Well, government is now slowly awakening to the challenge and opportunities in the corridor. Last year, the United States Congress authorized a pioneering international venture, the Cascadia Corridor Commission, to create a cross-border working alliance along the corridor to tackle transportation, conservation, economic diversification, technology, education and other challenges. The governments and the citizens in this Cascadia region now have to do the rest.

"There's a very strong basis for regional cooperation."

WILSON PARASIUK, Chairman and Chief Executive Officer, British Columbia Trade Development Corporation.

The report that Discovery Institute has done is excellent. I haven't seen anything like it for any other city in North America.

British Columbia and Washington state have much in common in terms of experiences, resources, and trading patterns. We both share the distinction of being probably the most exciting and dynamic growth areas in our respective countries. And these factors have begun to shape a definable region around us, which we might call Cascadia.

For example, trade between British Columbia and Washington and Oregon comes to an estimated $4.5 billion annually, and more than 20 million people per year cross between Washington and B.C. Our challenges, our opportunities, our outlooks are generally the same. So clearly, there's a very strong basis for regional cooperation. With our climate, our physical and human resources, our proximity to Asia Pacific, we will continue to attract population and generate economic activity. We have all become aware, however, of the costs that growth and development can exact on the environment and from human society. Clearly, growth does have its own side effects that aren't always the most functional.

Regional cooperation presents an opportunity to manage growth for the betterment of all. Recently the government of British Columbia put forward what's called the Georgia Basin Initiative, which is intended to address the effects of extremely rapid urban growth from the lower mainland of B.C.

Wilson Parasiuk

The challenge is to identify areas where cooperation will bring big mutual payoffs.

down through the Puget Sound area. We're talking about a population of 4.5 million that in the next 30 to 40 years could quite easily reach nine to 10 million, the population of Los Angeles. We would like that to happen without this area becoming a Los Angeles in terms of quality of life, safety, educational opportunities, and upward mobility. Those are very interesting challenges that we have to face. And yet, they are enviable challenges if you talk to people who live in Shanghai or Seoul or parts of Japan.

We've also had a number of other cooperative undertakings that jointly seek to respond to regional challenges. We have the Pacific Northwest Economic Partnership; the Pacific NorthWest Economic Region; the Pacific Corridor Enterprise Council; the Pacific Northwest Economic Conference; the B.C./ Washington Environment Cooperative Council; the Georgia Basin Initiative; the Cascadia Corridor Commission. All of these in their own right are good. In addition, we have a number of specific groups: the Pacific Northwest Industrial Council; the Western Forestry Conference; and a number of ad hoc committees relating to oil spills, science and technology, and environmental technology. Indeed, we may in fact have too many of these groups. Not everything has to be totally coordinated. We want some spontaneity and creativity.

Clearly the lesson of history is that cooperation works best when there is a demonstrable community of interest. And it's important to streamline this process and make it work well, because certainly British Columbia feels that there is a lot to be gained from cooperation with Washington state and with the Greater Seattle area.

We also have to recognize, however, that in many aspects, states and provinces and the cities within them can be intensely competitive. We have that in the commodities: lumber, wood, fish products, agricultural products. I don't think the port managers at Seattle and Tacoma and Vancouver are going to stop trying to capture each other's container business. And Sea-Tac and Vancouver Airport will not give each other one iota of market share. I would expect that Whatcom County, the county closest to British Columbia, will continue to try to entice B.C. companies to move over the border.

Now, that being said, they shouldn't be seen as insurmountable frictions. The challenge is to identify those areas where regional cooperation will really bring big mutual payoffs.

❏ One area where cross-border cooperation could bring positive results is in improving regional transportation links, especially with respect to intercity rail service. There has been some work done in improving access through the borders. We have to do much more to streamline that. But the rapid transit system based on rail holds a lot of promise for the corridor.

❏ Another natural area for regional cooperation is the development of the new knowledge-based industries. The foundations have already been laid through the Pacific Northwest Economic Partnership. This has encouraged companies in software development, biotechnology and environmental technology to explore areas for collaboration. Under the banner of this partnership, companies from Washington and B.C. have exhibited together at the Las Vegas COMDEX show for the last five years. Some of them have also jointly appeared at the CIBET trade show in Germany and participated in a mission to Japan. However, these have not been high-powered missions. The question is, can we move to that next level?

❑ We are both located on the rim of the Asia Pacific region. Without a doubt, it is the most dynamic area in the world economy. But we haven't even begun to take advantage of the enormous opportunities in Asia. Last year, Asian economies grew by an average of 8%, against overall world growth of less than 2%. With annual growth in the range of 12%, China is on track to becoming one of the world's largest economies within the next 25 years. We have the strength and advantages in this area of the globe that, if shared, will help us gain a position to profit from the tremendous growth in Asia.

Washington and B.C. have a combined population of eight million people and a total GDP in the range of $200 billion dollars. Add in Oregon, and the GDP climbs to $250 billion dollars, about the size of the Swedish economy. This gives us the critical mass to become visible and effective in the new world order, as noted by an article in *Business Week* published last year. The article, which grouped Washington, Oregon and B.C. as a region for high-tech growth, was instrumental in bringing a high-level economic mission from the Kansai region of Japan to Seattle and Vancouver last fall. This mission was going to visit Los Angeles and San Francisco, originally. They saw the article and decided to come up to Seattle and Vancouver. They found that people in Seattle and Vancouver seemed far more confident of their future than people in Los Angeles and San Francisco, and they became much more interested in this area.

Another advantage in Asian Pacific trade concerns our respective strengths. The size and penetration of major companies like Boeing and Microsoft is a tremendous advantage to Seattle. Meanwhile, Vancouver is emerging as a type of "Geneva of the Pacific"—as an international center for transporta-

tion, trade, travel and scholarship. We have a number of international institutions. We have an international financial center, an international commercial arbitration center, an international maritime center. We have the Asia Pacific Foundation. We have the Commonwealth of Distance Learning and the International Center for Criminal Justice. Our universities have extremely close links with Asian universities. The University of British Columbia alone has links with 35 Asian universities on a very

> ## *To become internationally oriented, we have to become much more cosmopolitan.*

intense working level. In addition, there are 70,000 graduates of Canadian universities who live in Hong Kong, because of the links we've had on the educational side. That is a tremendous set of networks.

Another advantage that Vancouver has is our large and dynamic Asian population. With a population of just over three million people in British Columbia, we have about 340,000 people of Asian descent living mostly in the Greater Vancouver area, many of whom come from Hong Kong or China. These people have considerable knowledge of and ties to markets and decision makers within Asia. A few years ago, no more than 500 students were learning Mandarin or Japanese in our schools. Today, 4,500 children are learning Mandarin and 3,500 are learning Japanese.

❑ A great deal can be gained from cooperation in promoting the Pacific Northwest region—Cascadia, as you call it—as an international destination for trade, investment and tourism. This would best be accomplished by encouraging pragmatic, workable and functional relations, and building from success to success. I'd like to propose working in three major areas: Two of these relate to high tech—one in the software area, and the second in environmental technologies. I'd like to see us organize a trade mission into Asia to deal with these two areas. The third area that is really important for us to work together is in tourism promotion. It's really important for people not just to think of Vancouver in a Canadian context or think of Seattle in an American context, but rather to think about how closely these two cities are to each other.

I want to conclude with a few harder questions: Do you really want to be a world-class city? We have this problem in Vancouver, as well. We're schizophrenic. We want the growth, we want the dynamism, we want the world-class status. That is, some of us want the growth and dynamism; some of us don't. There's a tug-of-war within British Columbia. I've heard comments, "Tell people it rains a lot here; therefore, we won't have more people come." It's reflective of a certain attitude. Do we want the newcomers to our area? Do we see the newcomers as assets or as interlopers? Do we want to know more about different parts of the world, especially Asia,

where the pace of change is geometric if not exponential? Or are we so ethnocentric that we assume that everyone, everywhere, drives on the right side of the road?

To become more internationally oriented, we have to become much more cosmopolitan. We have to become much more open-minded, more inquisitive, more tolerant and more visionary. This requires leadership at all levels of society, both public and private. But it also requires patience and perseverance. Attitudes don't change smoothly or easily. It's often easier to slip into chauvinistic or parochial postures when rough spots or backlash occur. At that time, it's just not enough to let a politician stand up and fight that. The whole society that cares about becoming an international cosmopolitan community has to stand up and be counted. I haven't seen enough of it yet in Vancouver, and I'm not sure you've seen enough of it yet here in Seattle to achieve what we all want to achieve.

7. What are the Obstacles to International Seattle and How Do We Overcome Them?

"Watch out that internationalism does not become a code word for certain hidden agendas."

DAVID BREWSTER, Editor-in-Chief and Publisher, Seattle Weekly.

As a card-carrying member of the New Pacific and of Cascadia, here are a few reservations that have occurred to me in reading the report and reacting to the comments of others.

First, on the question of tourism. I think that there is not a lot of grassroots interest in stimulating more tourism in this area, despite a lot of interest by those who would benefit by that. People in this area think of this as a nice place to live but you wouldn't want to visit there. We don't like the thought of it

being overrun with tourists and of competition for parks and natural areas. The true tourism to promote in this region is country tourism, sort of like New England. It's getting close to nature, bed and breakfasts, country inns, country resorts. When you put tourism into a broad state or whatever kind of entity that is promoting a region, you end up promoting the major economic interests—namely, large hotels, convention centers and cities. So it cuts against the kind of tourism that really would draw people here. I don't share the view that it's dumb for us not to be promoting this region nationally and internationally in tourism.

Another area where I differ with the report concerns the arts. If you think of the arts as an interna-

> *Most people around here do not believe in being an international city and in being a lot larger. They buy into "right size," not larger size.*

tional draw, you will distort the quality of the arts. International festivals are based on stars, on marquee value, on well-known works of arts, on celebrity art—not on more original art. It is very high priced, very risky. They can drag down local arts organizations by one miscalculation. And festival performances are typically not the highest level of art. They are under-rehearsed and they're put together in order to provide a highlight of somebody's vacation. Now, we can all think of exceptions to that—the Salzburg Festival is one example. But promoting our arts internationally, as a draw for tourism, is a dangerous path.

Another concern I have is how plausible really is the claim that this region (a) is a region and (b) is an international player? I don't think that most people think of themselves as living in Cascadia, of having a lot in common, even though you can cite a lot of things that we have in common. I don't think that we have a marketable uniqueness. No other region has this common identitiy either, particularly when you're talking about tourism and the arts. We also have, and the report cites some of these problems, a lack of financial institutions. We are remote from the national capital and remote from New York City and, therefore, somewhat remote from the discus-

sion of national and international issues.

The report seems to set up a situation where we can either go forward into internationalism or simply fall apart. I think there is some interesting middle ground. Most people around here do not believe in being an international city and in being a lot larger. They buy into "right size," not larger size; "steady state," not a highly cyclical and externally dependent economy.

There is a populist tradition in our politics here which fears and makes fun of pretension. You can see this over and over in the way the local media worries very much about whether President Gerberding of the University of Washington is making too much money or buying a carpet that's too expensive for his house. We talked before about sofas in the Port of Seattle. These are easy things to snipe at. But they do come from an anxiety about creating a city of long limousines, which may be the concern of going in that direction.

We believe that there is a proper carrying capacity to the land. We believe in being mid-sized, not Los Angeles-sized. We believe in having things which are affordable, not jacked up into the high price that a world city has. And we believe in being individualistic, rather than merging our identity into some broader, imperial overview. I would say that an effective model against the international one would think of this region as an incubator region—strong in research, creating a lot of industries, the Microsoft kind of culture. We create some companies, we lose some, but we still have the ground in which this is happening. That's a research-based, education-based, small-size, fast-on-its-feet incubation model as opposed to a larger city.

Watch out that internationalism does not become a code word for certain hidden agendas. Is it a device for rolling over obstructionists? Some of the report's language suggests that. As a veteran obstructionist, I object. Is it a pro-growth strategy, or is it neutral on that? Is it a way of putting a kind of fancy international French sauce over dubious local projects? Like the Denver airport: "We've got to have that, otherwise we'll lose." The close inspection of large capital projects is a great tradition in this region and you have to watch that you're not sweeping together things which really have nothing to do with internationalism.

And lastly, is the hidden agenda here to create or exacerbate the two-tier economy that Americans are very worried about anyhow? People living in penthouses in Seattle, moving a lot of businesses offshore, buying into an economy which seems to have the potential of being very difficult for people of moderate skills working with their hands. If so, there's going to be a strong resistance to that in Seattle, which has a strong social justice and social equity tradition. The report raises this question and then goes to the "rising tide lifts all boats" kind of argument. I think that we've had enough of that through the '80's to be skeptical.

Still, an important cultural shift is going on. This committee, this gathering, this report shows it. We are becoming, whether we want to or not, a world city. The real question is whether we want to simply allow that to continue to happen, which would be my argument, or whether we want to have a more interventionist, controlled, unified strategy. Good luck trying to get that, because this area is so devoted to processes that paralysis comes when you try to yoke together different governments, different interests, different classes, that want to assert their individualism.

The key is to limit the agenda, and do one or two highly visible projects. My two examples: a high-speed rail between Portland and Vancouver, which would do more than anything to enable ordinary people to feel that they are a part of this region. The other would be to create a free, unified higher-education zone, including British Columbia, Washington and Oregon. Any citizen in those two states and province could attend any of the universities at the same rate as if they lived in that state. Then apportion funds so that you can create an extraordinary medical school, an extraordinary architecture school, and so forth. That would do a lot to give people a feeling that they have gained by living in this region. It also would underscore that if we're going to be a research-based economy, we've got to have great research universities.

"Steps in the direction the report suggests would be healthy for this area…"

JAMES R. ELLIS, **Preston, Thorgrimson, Shidler, Gates & Ellis; founder of METRO.**

I have to say that I'm less afraid than David Brewster of an endless line of limousines in this town. I'm also less afraid of a successful French sauce over our Scandinavian background. In fact, I really have only one fear, and that is that this grand plan won't get any farther than this report.

It is very difficult to focus this metropolitan area on anything. It is extremely difficult to focus it on this agenda that we've described. It's fair to say we've got a lot of multiple goals for this region that can be summarized rhetorically as quality of life or a variety of other umbrella terms. But they require different actions, money and a lot of different kinds of leadership. I'm less concerned with the problem of identifying needs than with the horrendous problem of matching resources and needs and time and leadership. Those are extraordinarily difficult matches to make and without them, you simply have magnificent speeches. So, what's needed is a concerted effort by those interested in these goals to facilitate the efforts of overworked leaders. Not to capture them, but to make it a little easier for them to spend time and thought on this subject without telling them that they have to forget all the other important goals.

In defense of tourism, I find it easy to say that, when I go fishing, I don't want anybody else around in that particular stretch of stream. I've gotten past that because there are too many natives. There's no way that I can fish alone anymore, regardless of tourists. I see great value in tourism for all of us, and economic self-interest, if we do it intelligently. The need is to educate the local natives and to educate the Legislature in some pretty fundamental points. We can overstate the values of tourism, but we can also understate them. Tourists come here from out of state, they spend money here, but they're different from us. Tourists don't put their children in our schools. They don't populate our institutions. Schools and institutions are three-quarters of the general-fund budget. Tourists are on the plus side of the revenue stream in a sales-tax state, and you'd better treat them with some deference. So we have a unique resource and everyone who's thoughtfully examined this market understands the public value of that particular taxpayer who comes from out of the state.

And there's plenty of competition. We could easily raise our tax on tourists so far they wouldn't come here. We nearly have the highest hotel tax in the country now. We could make it prohibitive. In addition, there's business to be generated. I don't maintain that the average job in tourism pays as well as the average job at Boeing—about half as well, is what we could hope for. By the same token, we're looking at a shrinking manufacturing base and we will have to find ways of filling some of these gaps. Tourism strikes me as being an effective way of doing so. We need to invest in promotion and in attractions. We have beautiful natural attractions, many of which are accessible. It's one reason why I believe there are so many economic values to the Mountains-to-Sound Greenway; some of our most beautiful pieces of landscape are right at our doorstep. People can leave a hotel, ski at night, and come back to sleep. There are not too many places where

such things can happen. They can take a day trip to the coast. We have many day trips we offer people who come to meetings at the Convention Center. We say, stay, take your family, see Snoqualmie Falls.

James Ellis, Mike Fitzgerald, Carol Eastman

I learned a little bit about international tourism last year when I accidentally was in Snoqualmie in the middle of the "Twin Peaks Festival" and was totally surrounded by Japanese people who had been 747'd from Japan. I didn't believe it. It was such a large number of folks you couldn't move. And it's amazing what television advertising of Roslyn through "Northern Exposure" has done.

In short, the agenda of this report is absolutely excellent. I'm not worried that it's going to lead to us being the capital of the world. I do fear that it may simply drop out of sight, which would be par for the course, and I think that would be too bad. I think steps in the direction the report suggests would be healthy for this area, would strengthen us and will not lead to our total subversion.

"The idea of a ports merger should be put to rest."

PATRICK O'MALLEY, Commissioner, Port of Tacoma.

I fully appreciate the amount of work, the dedication and the labor that's been reflected in the draft report. Putting one of these things together is not a day at the beach, and it's a really comprehensive, excellent piece of work.

Having said that, I have four questions about the dreaded "m" word, which is the merger of the ports in Tacoma and Seattle:

First, is merger the only means to make Tacoma change market rates? Or, put in another way, as only David Brewster can do, is Tacoma "Puget Sound's Walmart"? In support of its argument for price cooperation, the draft suggests Tacoma's rates are too low compared to California's and this policy enables shipping companies to pit Seattle and Tacoma against each other. I believe this notion is naive for three reasons. First of all, price alone is an incomplete measure and one that I guarantee will lead to some false conclusions. It's clear you have to look at cost and service level in setting rates. For example, in Tacoma the Commission has always stressed high asset utilization as a policy. Of the 14 cranes at the Port of Tacoma, five are owned by our tenants. Seattle, on the other hand, owns 24 cranes. Container volume in each port is almost identical, about a million containers a year. New cranes are $7.5 million. All you have to do is figure out the arithmetic.

Secondly, availability of land must be considered in pricing. Until this year, the conventional wisdom in the port world was that terminal land was inelastic and that eventually Tacoma and Seattle would have a monopoly on rates. However, developments in Portland and Roberts Bank, Canada, are proof that the supply of terminal property in the Pacific Northwest is elastic. Thus, we'll never have a monopoly and Seattle and Tacoma should admit it and move on. In the past three years, Tacoma may have had an opportunity to increase its rates on one or two customers. Despite heated internal debate, we didn't do it.

However, merging ports because of one or two deals is short-sighted and ignores such developments as the emergence of the Puget Sound Ports Group. It also ignores the key fact that the container volume of each port is pretty much identical. Net operating income of Tacoma is $10 million, and has been $8-12 million over the last five or ten years. Seattle, on the other hand, has had losses as low as $5 million, and its highest net operating income is about $1 million. So there's a substantial difference there. And the Port of Seattle Commission is to be commended for the steps they're taking to change that. But in businesses with the scope of revenues that we have, that isn't going to turn around overnight.

Finally, Tacoma and Seattle's market share has dropped the last two years. I would ask, if we had been charging more through a merger, would our market share have been better? The answer's obvious. The draft report also suggests that pricing cooperation would lead to a far better return on investments in marine infrastructure. A number of years ago, a well-known Port of Seattle official observed that if this port really wanted to make money,

the best way to do it would be to turn the waterfront terminals near the Kingdome into condominiums. It is the most valuable waterfront north of San Francisco. I think it's important to balance our missions. On one hand, ports are here to assure a reasonable return on our taxpayers' investments. On the other hand, we're here to stimulate jobs and trade, and I don't think that's served by cooking our

Merging ports… is short-sighted and ignores such developments as the emergence of the Puget Sound Ports Group.

rates. The draft report notes that a combined Port Authority of Seattle and Tacoma would have been the second-largest container port in the United States. That's true. In my opinion, however, sheer size means little, which brings me to my second question: Is bigger really better? I frankly believe bigger isn't better and that it would merely create a suffocating bureaucracy.

A third question is from George Bush, about the "vision thing." Perhaps this comment is unduly harsh, and I don't mean it to be interpreted that way, but I offer it to show something about diversity in our region. The report leaves me with the impression that International Seattle would be some sort of a pasteurized, homogenized creation of marketing wizards. International Seattle residents would travel, study foreign languages and go to museums. They would enjoy ethnic cooking, as the report says, and they would be keenly aware of global interdependence. Well, maybe. But Tacoma's vision may be a little different. For one thing, I see working people who might not feel comfortable touring a museum or speaking French, but who know the value of a good job and enough about international trade to know that it's providing them with their bread and butter. And I see an area that is appealing to the international community, not because of some ingrained, harmonious qualities, but because the diversity is already there. Tacoma is a very different place from Seattle, just as Mercer Island is different from Puyallup and Kent and North Bend. We should capitalize on the differences.

Our ports are different, too, which brings me to the final question. Should we have a merger, or should we have an alliance based on cooperation? It's my position that the "m" word is history. Why is that? I spoke about the Puget Sounds Ports Group. Already six ports—Bellingham, Tacoma, Seattle, Everett, Olympia and Anacortes—have agreed to share multi-year capital, comprehensive and budget plans. In addition, a strategy for increasing tourism, utilization of existing port facilities and Puget Sound's share of trade flows will be developed. No other port group in the United States or North America has agreed to such an endeavor. The ports should be congratulated for their initiative. In addition, there is already well advanced in planning, an exciting Russian trade project with private-sector participation this fall. And that's just the beginning.

However, whenever a Seattle-Tacoma merger was proposed, during the two years that we've been meeting on a monthly or bimonthly basis, creative thinking came to a halt. That's because merger always has been a divisive issue among our ports and our communities. So I'd like to suggest that the idea of a ports merger should be put to rest. Let's stop wasting precious time on it. We should focus on ideas that will move us forward, not backward, because the opportunities are too exciting. After two years our cooperative efforts have landed the 1995 conference of the International Association of Ports and Harbors. This convention will bring 850 to 1,000 port officials from around the world to Seattle and they will visit ports in Puget Sound as well. Tacoma and Seattle should focus on why the rail cost for a container to Toronto is several hundred dollars less out of LA and Long Beach than it is from Puget Sound. And once we figure it out, we should try to do something to address that.

And finally, China's exports rose 22%, to $85 million, and imports grew 27%, to $81 billion in 1992. For 1993, China trade is expected to reach $200 billion. What does that mean to ports? Simply this: Seattle and Tacoma both have extensive Sister Port relationships in China. We have one in Tianjin in Northern China, which is the gateway to Beijing. Seattle has one in Shanghai. The ports should look at what we can build together that will be market-driven and not just warm handshakes and some receptions. If we focus on market-driven projects and not divisive, interregional issues, the sky's the limit.

[Authors' Note: As the final report notes, the "merger" proposal has been dropped!]

"There isn't a U.S. economy, or a Pacific Northwest economy. It's now a global economy…"

MIKE FITZGERALD, Director, Wash. State Dept. of Trade and Economic Development.

I want to commend Bruce and John for their vision, tenacity, and perseverance, to take what was a kernel of an idea, talk to hundreds of people on this issue, and bring us together to refocus and reposition ourselves. You can find publications that are 60, 70 years old that talk about this being the Pacific Gateway, the land of opportunity, the trade center of the Pacific Coast. People have been thinking about this for a long time. And a lot has been done. We're at a new epoch now.

But what will it take to now move to action? Clearly, education is going to be the key. We need to move expeditiously to make sure we have really international education for our children here. What we achieve from this time forward is going to depend on our ability to get things done as measured by world standards. Technology is the great equalizer in the global economy. Technology is to the global economy what the Colt 45 was to the West. If you've got it, you're on par with everybody else, particularly if you know how to wield it. If we have a population that understands how the world works, that thinks like global citizens, that knows how to wield technology, we have access to the best teachers in the world, we have access to our business partners anywhere in the world 24 hours a day.

The kind of world that's already evolved, not in the year 2000, not the 21st Century, but now, is a world where borders matter less and less and less. There isn't a U.S. economy, or a Pacific Northwest economy. It's now a global economy in which we're trying to assess what our strengths are and how to build upon those to position ourselves—and for what?

Economic development, trade, education, transportation—these are means to an end. What is the end? That together we are going to have to define.

It's some kind of quality of life, some kind of standard of living, some kind of political entity that we want to evolve to give all of our citizens the opportunity, the capacity, the place and a way to realize our potential.

For the first time since the Industrial Revolution began, what now constitutes a good business climate is the same list that constitutes a good quality of living climate. It's no different. High quality education, first-class infrastructure, excellent government services. You make the list: recreation, cultural opportunities, a high educational and a high tolerance level, multi-cultural citizens who think like world citizens. It's the same. That reality should inform our private investment decisions and our political decisions from this time forward.

8. What Role Can the University of Washington Play in International Seattle?

"We recognize that an international mission and strategy is needed."

CAROL EASTMAN, Vice Provost and Dean, Graduate School, University of Washington.

When I read the draft report, I was amazed as to how close it is to what we're finally ready to do with regard to international education. At the University, I'm Dean of the Graduate School and Vice Provost, but part of my portfolio is now international affairs and programs. And I was very pleased to see that this was overtly called for. There are a number of international programs already in place that are strong, but there is a feeling on campus, among students, faculty and staff, and in the community, that the university needs to be doing a much better job of coordinating and focusing its international activities. Efforts on campus often seem fragmented, uncoordinated. There's no idea of who's in charge.

We now have a preamble to our draft international mission and strategy statement. In it we say that the university will avow its commitment to strengthening the international dimensions of all aspects of its overall mission, teaching, research and community service. We recognize that an international mission and strategy is needed.

What might this mean in practice?

A recent language task force report urged that educators, state and nationwide, work toward a coherent educational policy with regard to foreign-language education. This should be language and culture education from kindergarten through graduate school. What this means is that the UW should work with other interested constituents in the state to lobby for early-start language instruction. Internally on campus, departments involved in language teaching need to work more effectively with our College of Education to improve student training. And since teachers need certification, that ought to require some schooling in the language and culture of countries involved.

However, it's clear that there's a major role for education in many arenas other than language to play in the context of developing an international Seattle. From the start, the university's international education effort has to have groundwork laid in the K-12 system. As the university develops what it's calling an international mission and strategy, it is not oblivious to the need for public and private schools in the city and the state to internationalize their curricula.

On campus we agree that the university needs a stronger commitment to study-abroad programs. Now the majority of students who study abroad go to Western Europe. It's very important that we find ways for these students to study in Pacific Rim countries as well as in other parts of the world. Funding is a key issue, since most of the students who participate in study-abroad programs pay their own way. It's most important that students need to learn the value of international education before they come to the university.

We also see a link between international studies and multi-cultural studies. UW students need to be able to see themselves as others see them and to understand others in relation to themselves. When we go out and recruit faculty and students we have to pay more attention to their international and interdisciplinary interests. Of critical import is for us to increasingly recognize international activities when it comes to rewarding faculty, when we evaluate them for promotion and merit increases. Special funding for international travel, for acquiring international databases, for purchasing international journals, for setting up infrastructures for exchange agreements and for developing international research grant proposals needs to be found.

With regard to international studies at the university, location seems to be the critical driver for developing our mission and our international strategy. We have access to the Pacific Rim; we also have 1,500 students on campus from these countries. We are cognizant of the dynamism of Asian economies and the strength we already have in Asian studies.

It should come as little surprise that the university's international mission and strategy is one which we are calling "Global Vision with an Asian Tilt." To fulfill this mission, it's necessary for us to develop and nurture partnerships internally and externally. We're beginning to work toward developing partnerships with foreign universities and with our alumni associations in a number of major cities, especially in Asia.

9. What Can the State Do to Promote International Seattle?

"We recognize the importance of trade and being globally competitive."

GOVERNOR MIKE LOWRY, State of Washington.

First, I want to thank the Discovery Institute and the individuals involved— Bruce Chapman and John Hamer, our friend John Miller and others— for the recognition of how important it is that we view ourselves as a region within the global economy and work to increase our global competitiveness. I am going to confine my remarks to the particular state role. We recognize the importance of trade and being globally competitive. That is a high priority of our efforts in Olympia. Mike Fitzgerald at what will be our Department of Community, Trade and Economic Development, is leading us forward, even in this very difficult state budget time.

In terms of efficiencies and consolidations in state government, if you set aside higher education, we will have an increase in the number of FTE's (Full-Time Employees), because we're adding 10,000 more students to the higher-education rolls. Very few things will be more important to global competitiveness than to have the highest quality possible higher education. If you add 10,000 students, that does take some more professors.

I'm happy to report with this budget, we have a 50% increase in state dollars for tourism. No longer will we continue to be 49th in the country. And I absolutely agree with the effort to homeport cruise ships for that great Alaska trade. And even with these deep cuts, we have expanded our trade operations into other localities around the world. We now will have a Russian Trade Office. We will be developing ways to work in Mexico, which is critically important. And we have not only kept but expanded our offices in Taiwan, Japan and Europe.

But what is the important state role beyond that? First and foremost is the quality of our education, the quality of our workforce. We have to have the best education, best prepared workforce, to be able to compete. There's only two things that aren't really transferable within the global economy, and that's the quality of the workforce and the infrastructure on which your economy operates.

And even though we're having these budget cuts, we put money into those programs that will advance education reform. We must be doing much more to communicate globally, by teaching foreign languages. We made that investment even in this tough time. And we strengthened the higher-education system in the state. Compare that to our friends to the south. In Oregon, education systems are being decimated because of the myopic Proposition 5 tax rollback, which will be one of the worst things that ever happened in that state. There's no way you can compete globally and wipe out your

education system. There's talk about closing an entire college. It's even worse in California, where perhaps the single worst thing happening could be the decimation of the California higher-education system. We will pay for that as a country greatly. The state of Washington is not going to make that penny-wise and pound-foolish mistake.

Another area that the state has a very critical role in is infrastructure. Mobility is critical to being a global competitor. What in the world is trade if it's

Governor Mike Lowry

We must dedicate ourselves to an integrated transportation system.

not mobility? And we sit here as the fifth-most-congested area in the United States. It often takes an apple truck longer to go from Issaquah to the Port of Seattle than it does from Wenatchee to Issaquah. In the year 2010 the average speed in King County will be 14 miles per hour. We have got to realize that if we're going to be internationally competitive we must understand the importance of mobility. We must dedicate ourselves to an integrated transportation system that gets us mobility, from air transport to sea transport to ground transport. And if we continue to have ourselves stopped by saying, "My gosh, don't raise my gas tax a couple of pennies," if we continue the politics of avoidance, of not making the investments necessary for mobility, then we are not meeting our responsibilities in a global economy.

10. How Can the Federal Government Help International Seattle?

"We must all cooperate to identify creative ways in which the federal goverment can help."

U.S. SENATOR SLADE GORTON.

Two years ago Bruce Chapman and John Hamer invited me to a roundtable discussion of the proposal that has become the International Seattle report. At that time, I said I saw a very limited role for the federal government in promoting metropolitan Seattle as a more globally competitive international city. One of my reasons was the view my colleagues in the U.S. Senate had of our area. Two years ago, when my colleagues looked at Seattle and Puget Sound, they saw an area unaffected by recession. They saw Boeing and its tremendous backlog of orders for new planes. They saw the emergence and strong growth of Microsoft, McCaw, Immunex and other high-tech and biotech firms. My colleagues knew the trade opportunities created by the Seattle and Tacoma Ports. In short, my colleagues viewed Puget Sound as an already incredibly competitive global city. It would be unreasonable to expect that Senators from economically depressed states would vote or act to help metropolitan Seattle become more globally competitive. While most of my colleagues still envy the state which I represent, the luster has dimmed. The recession has hit the Northwest, with Boeing and other businesses laying off workers.

I still believe that the federal government will and should play only a limited role in creating a more globally competitive metropolitan Seattle. But we must all cooperate to identify creative ways in which the federal government can help. Our Congressional delegation should act as ambassadors to the federal government and to foreign governments as well. The Goodwill Games is a good example of that role. A more recent example was the recruitment of Nintendo of America to become owners of the Mariners. Delegation members can convince members of the Administration and distinguished academicians and professionals to visit and attend conferences in our area. Finally, they can act to attract new consulates to our area and prevent existing ones from closing. And just as importantly, our Congressional delegation should ensure that Congress and the Administration pursue federal policies that help our region. Fighting fiercely for the policies that allow firms to compete abroad is our absolute responsibility as a Congressional delegation, because no region in the United States stands to gain so much from free trade as the Pacific Northwest, and no region will suffer as severely from protectionism. GATT and NAFTA have the potential for expanding our markets and setting promising precedents for freer trade. However, attitudes in Washington, D.C., about GATT and NAFTA, ranging from indifference to hate, threaten us with the possibility of trade contraction in our region, an event that perhaps more than all of our federal proposals for spurring this economy could slow our region's growth and subvert the goals that you are discussing today. We can also offer critical support in the areas of transportation, high-speed rail, adequate port facilities and infrastructure for cross-country shipments, all of which will help sustain our area's continued growth.

In these processes, we as a Congressional delegation must consider the views of the Northwest interest groups. Fortunately, we represent a highly skilled, forward-looking workforce that has remained at the cutting edge of our country's development, and I'm confident that the policies that help our region are generally good for the country.

Epilogue

Looking to the Future

Leadership is crucial.

Individuals, working alone or through their company, non-profit organization or government office, will make the difference in determining whether metropolitan Seattle develops its international interests in an unplanned, casual way, or pursues a loosely coordinated strategy like that recommended here, or tries to repudiate the internationalization trend altogether. People being people, there certainly will be forces pushing in all these directiions.

Most likely, we will see drift, decision and reaction combined in terms of Seattle's internationalist destiny; shambling growth, thoughtful growth and destructive negatavism all in play at the same time. The question is, what will be the overall trend?

To know the answer to that question is to ask another first: Will the metropolitan area allow leadership to manifest itself on this and other subjects? Leaders do not require supine acceptance of their initiatives by the rest of us; it is imperative that we debate the proposals made at any level of community action and consider costs and benefits and rational alternatives. That is why the arguments and proposals made in Parts I and II of this book were, in their initial condition, subjected to the criticism and suggestions of hundreds of people (as indicated in Part III), and then revised accordingly.

But, leadership is crucial.

We suggest that the constituency most in need of a voice right now is the largely inarticulate body of support for internationalism—the people who, for whatever reason, realize the enormous significance of foreign trade and the need for a network of support for internationalism generally. (That is true nationally as well as in our region, by the way.) If supporters of internationalism, knowing the stakes for our economy, educational system and quality of life, have a voice, they should be asking their public officials: How do you stand on this question? What are you doing to make metropolitian Seattle more competitive (that is, more successful) in the international marketplace?

Today, those questions are still seldom asked. Individual leaders step forward in this field, as in others, not because they are responding to expressed public opinion but because they have a sense of how our future must develop if we are to avoid either ruinous bad growth or economic stagnation. But these leaders are up against the easy thrills available to the negatavist, who is ever eager to complain about society's failures and even quicker to attack attempts to create a positive consensus.

When, after the Gold Rush, Seattle leaders sponsored the Alaska-Pacific-Yukon Exposition, which perhaps marks the first expression of an internationalist destiny for this area, there must have been nay-sayers, even though it was a boosterish age. There certainly were vocal skeptics when, in the early 1960's, a few enlightened leaders, most of them from the private sector initially, launched Century 21, the Seattle World's Fair, which, among other things, pushed Seattle a generation ahead in the arts, and left us all the facilities and continuing potential of Seattle Center. Indeed, the same kind of doubt threatened to swamp Spokane's World's Fair, a number of years later, and nearly rode down the early enthusiasm for the Goodwill Games in Seattle in the last decade.

None of that doubting attitude was very original; skepticism, even cynicism, was not invented in Seattle, and there is probably less of it here than elsewhere. We also have to admit that good plans need good critics to force efforts to correct and improve.

The trouble is that being a skillful public negatavist

may be seen by some these days as a more acceptable role than being a positive leader. We *use* negatavists, even if we do not admire them; leaders somehow seem to frighten and intimidate us. Before they get very far, we not only try to refute their ideas, or defeat them, but we find ways to challenge their personal integrity and decency and even to put their livelihood and legal security at risk. The ancient Athenians used to banish their leaders; we merely banish them in place.

But somehow, people still do offer their time and their reputations into the service of their city, and that is still more true in our area than elsewhere. What the pioneers called "The Seattle Spirit"—the willingness to work out the problems and, in good cheer, move ahead together—miraculously survives. Several independent initiatives are underway in Seattle that point us to a strategy for our area that either exemplify the international strategy (and they have been noted throughout this report) or are entirely compatible with it (such as the Seattle Commons). The *leaders* of these projects have us in their debt, whether we ever say thanks or not.

But for the larger picture, we also remember that The Seattle Spirit always prevailed only when enthusiasm and civic duty were both joined and *organized*. Discovery Institute has emphasized in the book you have just read the key step of institutionalizing the international program: providing in one place a voluntary coordinating center and information clearinghouse for the private, non-profit (volunteer) and governmental sectors. If, for the first time in this country, at least, that mechanism can be perfected—as now seems possible—a long parade of progress in this community will form up.

The international civic strategy for Seattle is far stronger than it was even a year ago. Our relative success is attracting attention in other parts of the United States and Canada. We should take pride in that and do all we can to help other communities. But first, we need to create more sustained support here.

Leadership *is* crucial.

Project Advisory Board

JEFF DEMETRESCU, *Director, Market and Targeted Industry Development, Washington State Department of Trade and Economic Development.*

FRANK DILLOW, *Director, Government Affairs, GTE Northwest.*

RICHARD J. ELLINGS, *Executive Director, National Bureau of Asian Research.*

DON EZRA, *Senior Vice President, Frank Russell Co.*

MIKE FITZGERALD, *Director, Washington State Department of Trade and Economic Development.*

RIO HOWARD, *Business Development Specialist, Port of Seattle.*

PING KIANG, *Partner, Perkins Coie.*

MEGAN KRUSE, *Editor, Pacific Rim Entrepreneur.*

PATRICK KUO, *President, Cascadia Development Corp.*

DON LORENTZ, *Director, Economic and Trade Development, Port of Seattle.*

HELEN I . MARIESKIND, *President, Sime Health Limited.*

RAOUL MEILLEUR, *Director, International Programs, Bellevue Community College.*

SUSAN MOCHIZUKI, *Executive Director, Japan America Society.*

STEVE MORRIS, *President/CEO, Seattle-King County Convention and Visitors Bureau.*

DAN NYE, *Partner, Riddell Willilams Bullitt & Walkinshaw.*

JOHN OPPENHEIMER, *President, Columbia Resource Group.*

ROBIN PASQUARELLA, *Executive Director, Henry M. Jackson Foundation.*

DAN RAMIREZ, *Executive Director, Redmond Chamber of Commerce.*

MICHAEL SANDLER, *Partner, Foster Pepper & Shefelman.*

PAUL SCHELL, *Commissioner, Port of Seattle; Dean, University of Washington College of Architecture and Urban Planning.*

BILL STAFFORD, *Executive Director, Trade Development Alliance of Greater Seattle.*

LIZ THOMAS, *Legislative Aide to King County Councilman Ron Sims.*

TOM TIERNEY, *Director, Seattle Office of Intergovernmental Relations.*

RAY WALDMANN, *Corporate Director, Federal Affairs, The Boeing Company.*

Acknowledgments

Discovery Institute Fellows, staff and volunteers who have contributed enormously to this project include John G. West, Jr., Diane Hodgson, Ellen Pritchard-Silvey, Kathryn Flower, Margie Wickham, Shannon Boldizsar, Teresa Gonzales, Jim Quitslund, George Gilder, and Paul Fleming. Tieta Ralston, a graduate student at the University of Washington's Jackson School of International Studies, has been invaluable as an international research assistant, thanks to a grant from the Henry M. Jackson Foundation.

The report was designed by John G. West, Jr., and charts and graphs were created by Bill Hankes of Perkins Coie. In addition, the following organizations supplied photos for the report: Port of Seattle (pp. 1, 30); Seattle-King County Convention and Visitors Bureau (pp. 23, 56); *The Blaine Banner* (p. 28); University of Washington (pp. 37, 38, 47); Washington State Convention and Trade Center (p. 43); and Seattle Art Museum (p. 57). Photographer Kevin Morris supplied pictures of the International Seattle conference contained in part three of the report. And the Port of Seattle supplied the photo that appears on the cover.

About Discovery Institute

Discovery Institute is a Seattle-based public policy center for national and international affairs, which has been in independent operation since 1991. Our programs proceed from what most citizens consider the sound principles of representative democracy, individual liberty, free enterprise, technological advancement, regional cooperation, and internationalism.

Most of Discovery Institute's support comes from foundation and corporate funding for particular projects or subject areas, as well as substantial in-kind gifts and services. However, Discovery is also a membership organization. Individuals, businesses, and foundations that provide general suppport regularly receive briefings on public issues through our various publications. By participating in Discovery Institute, members assist our independent, nonpartisan work and help themselves to stay current with developments in public policy fields important to them and their communities.

About the Authors

Bruce Chapman, President of Discovery Institute, is a former U.S. Ambassador, Deputy Assistant to the President, Director of the U.S. Census Bureau, Washington State Secretary of State, and Seattle City Councilmember. He is also the co-author of *The Party That Lost Its Head* and author of *The Wrong Man in Uniform*.

John Hamer, Senior Fellow at Discovery Institute and director of the International Seattle project, is a former Associate Editorial Page Editor for *The Seattle Times* and former Associate Editor of *Editorial Research Reports*, a publication of *Congressional Quarterly*.

For further information, please call or write:

Discovery Institute
1201 Third Avenue, 40th floor
Seattle, WA 98101-3099
Telephone: (206) 287-3144
Telefax (206) 583-8500

In addition to the grant provided by Key Bank for publication of this report, major funding for the International Seattle project, which led to this report and to a conference in May 1993, was provided by

BOEING & Port of Seattle

Further support of the International Seattle project came from:

AT&T
Browning Ferris Industries, Inc.
Cascadia Hospitality Management Co.
Foster, Pepper & Shefelman
GTE Northwest, Inc.
Heller, Ehrman, White & McAuliffe
The Henry M. Jackson Foundation
KIRO Broadcasting
McCaw Cellular Communications, Inc.
The Medina Foundation
LIN Broadcasting
Lufthansa German Airlines
Paul Schell Associates
PEMCO Financial Center
Perkins Coie
Riddell, Williams, Bullitt & Walkinshaw
Seafirst Bank
Third Avenue Productions
US West
Washington State Department of Trade & Economic Development
Wright Runstad & Co.